A *QUIET MIND* COMPANION

A *QUIET MIND* COMPANION

*A Personal Journey in the
Light of White Eagle's Teaching*

JENNY DENT

THE WHITE EAGLE PUBLISHING TRUST
NEW LANDS : LISS : HAMPSHIRE : ENGLAND

First published 1993
Reprinted 1995

© *Copyright, Jenny Dent, 1993*

British Library Cataloguing-in-Publication Data
A catalogue record for this book is available
from the British Library
ISBN *0-85487-091-1*

Printed in Great Britain
at the University Press, Cambridge

CONTENTS

6

ACKNOWLEDGMENTS

My first acknowledgment is to that beautiful ray of pure light, love and wisdom which has been brought by 'White Eagle'. I thank all my family for their love and support and sharing of the path with me: my parents, my husband Geoffrey, and children Sara and Michael. I want to give special thanks to my dear 'sister' and colleague Anna Hayward, for her many helpful suggestions and encouragement in the preparation of the manuscript. I thank Graham Browne who led the 'Self-Transformation Courses' I attended in 1985–86 which changed my life and opened so many new windows in my understanding. I also want to thank Patricia Fletcher for her patient typing, and Colum Hayward for all his editorial assistance.

I am grateful to Hazel Smith for permission to use the words by her mother, Pat Cooke, on page 24, and to the various friends and correspondents whose letters I have quoted.

The portion from A COURSE IN MIRACLES is © copyright, 1975 and reprinted by permission of the Foundation for Inner Peace, Inc., P. O. Box 1104, Glen Ellen, California 95442, and Penguin Books, London. I am also grateful to Pat Rodegast and Bantam Books for permission to use three quotations from EMMANUEL'S BOOK and EMMANUEL'S BOOK II; to Steven Foster and Meredith Little and Rites of Passage Press, Big Pine, California, for the quotation from THE SACRED MOUNTAIN: A VISION QUEST HANDBOOK FOR ADULTS; to Peter Owen Publishers, London, for the extract from SIDDHARTHA by Hermann Hesse; and to HarperCollins, London, and Judith Blackstone and Zoran Josipovic, the authors of ZEN FOR BEGINNERS, for the quotations from their book which I have used.

PREFACE

THE QUIET MIND has been sold all over the world and is now published in twelve different languages*. At the headquarters of the White Eagle Lodge in England, we receive letters telling of the transforming effect of the White Eagle teaching. Many mention the sayings in THE QUIET MIND and tell stories of the often-extraordinary ways it came into their hands; of how they were 'guided' to pick it up in a bookshop, or a friend was 'led' to give it to them. Many people have expressed sentiments similar to those of a recent letter which reads: 'We are going through a testing time at the moment and I believe it is White Eagle's THE QUIET MIND that is keeping me sane.'

This 'Companion' has been born out of a series of articles I based around that book, entitled 'Making It Work For You', which appeared some years ago in the White Eagle magazine STELLA POLARIS. More recently I have started to lead groups on the theme of 'Healing Relationships in the Light of White Eagle's Teaching', and some of the ideas for these have germinated alongside the work I have done turning those articles into this much fuller book. Doing so has been instructive for me, and I hope that what has come up will be of value to you too.

The theme of healing relationships recurs frequently in my work and I hope to develop it further in the years ahead.

* Czech, Danish, Dutch, French, German, Japanese, Mexican Spanish, Norwegian, Portuguese, Brazilian Portuguese, Swedish and of course English

HOW TO USE THIS BOOK

I have not wanted to make this a 'work-book' (with any feeling of pressure about 'having to do something' in order to get a particular result), but nevertheless it is intended to be a very practical one—a book to use as an aid to daily aspiration, rather than for mental study. I hope it will be a tool to help set you free to grow in awareness of your own perfection: what in Buddhist terminology is your 'Buddha nature' and in Christian, your divinity or 'Christhood'. If this linking of two such different religions surprises you I will explain right away that for me the White Eagle teaching draws together many different threads from all the religions of the world, all of which have their origin in the age-old Ancient Wisdom. Every one of them has its own unique gift to offer us.

The chapters of the book are based on the nine chapters of THE QUIET MIND. At the beginning of each, I have shared some of my own and others' experience in following the White Eagle teaching. I have then gone on to give practical suggestions about ways to help ourselves 'make it work for us', including a visual meditation on the theme and ideas for affirmations. None of this is intended as a rigid formula which we are supposed to follow in order to reach a particular goal. Having both Sun and Mars in Aries, I am naturally 'goal-oriented', but I have been working recently on letting go of goals and rigid agendas, to allow more space for spontaneity and unexpected delight, and for growing in awareness that everything (including myself and everyone else) is *perfect right now*—a theme I shall explain and develop.

As I was brought up in the White Eagle work, the six-pointed star has become an integral part of my life and work (see the section that follows, 'Who is White Eagle?') and I have developed its symbolism a little at a time as the book progresses. I have found it a constant inspiration. Every year that passes I become aware of more meaning in the star symbol and each chapter ends with an interpretation of the six-pointed star as it relates to that chapter's theme.

Throughout the book I discriminate between the experience of the 'little self' and that of the 'Christ-self' or 'true self' (what is sometimes called the 'higher self'). It is always difficult to find the best words to convey spiritual concepts, and we can often be put off by unfamiliar jargon. I hope the terms I have chosen will not jar and will be helpful. The 'Christ-self' is our complete self, our perfection, our Buddha nature, our oneness in God and the sum of all we have built into our souls through many incarnations. The 'little self' is the everyday personality, the 'uncut jewel' upon which we are working in this lifetime. This personality has within it many pieces of work that are unfinished from past lives, which surface for our attention at different periods in our lifetime.

Two more terms which may need clarifying are 'Master' and 'Teacher'. White Eagle refers often to 'the Master' in THE QUIET MIND, and we are given the vision of the qualities of the master soul. When he refers to 'the Master' he is not referring exclusively to a personality, but rather allowing the term to mean 'the illumined soul', the fully realized human being. If we wish, we can think of 'the Master' as being a particular sainted one with whom we feel an affinity, such as Jesus, or Gautama Buddha. The term 'teacher' can be synonymous with 'master', or it can refer to our own individual spirit guide, who is often a disciple of the master with whom we feel affinity.

Page references given in the text are to THE QUIET MIND itself (except at chapter openings); biblical quotations, common in extracts from White Eagle's teaching, are italicized.

WHO IS WHITE EAGLE?

If you are not familiar with the White Eagle Lodge and the teaching therein you may be wondering 'Who is White Eagle?' The answer may at first puzzle you. Although we think of White Eagle as a distinct personality, he tends to imply that he would prefer to lay his personality on one side and remind us that he is the spokesman for a group, often referred to as the White Brotherhood. Our desire to define personalities is very human, very earthly. Maybe as you read you will begin to get a sense of what happens when the distinctions and labels of personality are softened. White Eagle is still 'dear old White Eagle', but he is also a loving emanation, a ray of the star which carries a greater sense of the love at the heart of things than any physical personality could. However, we do have a little booklet (with the same title as this section, 'Who is White Eagle?') which puts together some of the things he himself has said which gives at least a sketch of the wise teacher whom we have come to know so well.

The teaching which is printed in the White Eagle books and in THE QUIET MIND was channelled by my grandmother Grace Cooke. She died in 1979, but the work which the teaching inspired has grown year by year. White Eagle has continued to guide and inspire this work through our present-day leaders, Grace Cooke's daughters, Joan Hodgson and Ylana Hayward.

White Eagle has always said that he is working on the ray of St John (whose symbol is an eagle) and that the wise brothers in the inner world for whom he speaks are working to help humanity through 'the years of fire'—the time of transition between the old age of Pisces and the new Aquarian age, the age of brotherhood. The symbol of the group is the six-pointed star, and they inspired the foundation of the Polaire Brotherhood, which subsequently became the White Eagle Star Brotherhood. Its work—to project the Christ healing light into our world, using the star symbol as a focal point—continues to be the central work of the White Eagle Lodge.

When White Eagle was working with my grandmother he chose to use one of his past-life personalities predominantly, that of the Iroquois chief. But he can truly appear in any 'dress'. I have seen him as a Zen teacher, a Chinese philosopher, and even in a modern business suit. Usually, when I see him, he appears to me clothed in a simple white Grecian-type robe. The thing that is most remarkable about him is his twinkling blue eyes and wonderful sense of humour.

*

Maybe you already know and love THE QUIET MIND and have been using it for many years, or maybe it is new to you, or this is your first introduction to the White Eagle teaching. But however this *QUIET MIND* COMPANION has come to you, and at whatever stage in your contemplation and use of THE QUIET MIND itself, I hope it will prove of value in your life and help you make the White Eagle teaching a practical, loving reality.

INTRODUCTION TO *THE QUIET MIND*

A GENTLE BROTHER

It is no good listening to White Eagle or to any other teacher unless you yourself work for self-mastery. The beginning of this work is your awareness of the still small voice within, of that gradually increasing Light in you which causes you to react as a gentle brother to all the conditions and all the circumstances of life.

The above words come in chapter two of THE QUIET MIND. Each of our chapters will begin with a similar seed-thought, and this one is in a sense the theme of my book. In fact, in the introductory section of the book we are given a vision of just such a gentle brother of the spirit which helps us see what it is that we are growing towards:

> If you can think of yourself as being all that you know you should be: constant, gentle, loving and kind to every man, woman and child, and to every circumstance in life; kind and tolerant in your attitude towards all conditions on earth; above all, if you can conceive yourself as being completely calm in all conditions and circumstances, quiet and yet strong—strong to aid your weaker brethren, strong to speak the right word, to take the right action, and so become a tower of strength and light; if you can see yourself facing injustice

17

and unkindness with a serene spirit, knowing that all things work out in time for good, and that justice is always eventually triumphant; if you have patience to await the process of the outworking of the will of God: if you can picture becoming like this, you will know something of mastership. (p. 8)

At first reading this may seem so far removed from how we see ourselves right now that we cannot believe in our ever coming near what White Eagle describes. However, he gives us a vision of God's perfection manifesting in human life, and encourages us to believe in our own divinity. Time and again he chides us gently for believing that we are 'only human': not so, he would say, you are first and foremost divine beings, 'spirit first and body last' (p. 14).

He knows life in a physical body can be tough, however, and he helps us to realize how important it is for us to be able to feel okay about how we are right here and now. It is all too easy to forget the part of ourselves which is divine. Usually we have to keep on reminding ourselves. It is because we are divine that we are also perfect, in our true God-selves. The 'little self' of our everyday personality is like a child; it is headstrong and untutored. But the wise parent knows how to bring the best out of a child, partly through gentle discipline, but even more through unconditional loving and understanding. The more we can be the wise parent to our little self, the more we can help that self to become whole, and wholeness means full awareness of our divinity, our oneness with God.

When Buddha attained enlightenment it is said that he exclaimed with delight at realizing that all beings are inherently enlightened; they just don't know it. It is only our own confusion which stops us realizing our natural wisdom and goodness. The same truth is inherent in White Eagle's teaching, and he seeks to remove this confusion and constantly encourages us on our path. He advises us not to dwell on past mistakes or our inadequacies and seeming failures. Instead, when we feel we could have done better, he suggests that we quietly acknowledge this to ourselves, make the clear intention to do it differently next time, and then move forward with a joyous, light heart. He assures us we are never alone in our endeavours. If we need help on our journey, it is always there:

> If you will be steadfast on the path to which your feet have been guided, you will find the treasure of life, a never-ending stream of help and healing and happiness. We, your brothers and guides, are on the road by your side. Not one of you stands alone. You have only to ask in simple trust, and you shall receive; whatever your need, it shall be supplied. (p. 11)

I hope this book will fulfil some need for you and be an additional companion on your path, and an encouragement in your endeavour to become 'a gentle brother'.

1

THE MASTER SOUL IS CONSTANT

If you can keep your certain, sure contact with God, nothing can go wrong in your life. You have no need to worry about decisions whether to do this, that or the other. Your decisions will be made for you, but you must be awakened to the spirit, quickened in spirit, so that you will instantly respond to the gentle guidance of the almighty Presence within you.

THROUGHOUT his teaching White Eagle reminds us of our need to withdraw a little from the clamours of material life, so that we may become more aware of the strength and help which is *inside* us. Too often we allow ourselves to become so busy with material concerns that we cut ourselves off from our source of help—God's light within—help which is always there, and will never let us down. It is truly our own salvation. 'You are spirit first and body last', says White Eagle (p. 14); but usually we forget spirit entirely, or feel that it is more the other way round. The 'gravitational pull of earthiness' (to use White Eagle's own phrase) is very strong and, especially if our bodies are feeling tired or sick, it is particularly difficult to have any awareness at all of our spiritual being. Yet White Eagle loves and encourages us all the time, and shows us simple ways in which we can work on ourselves, for his advice is always simple and practical. He tells us that we get too concerned about trivialities, and that we need to let them recede so that we can reconnect with God's love. He reminds us that 'the way to pray is to put yourself into complete attunement with the spirit of love' (p. 14), and he points out that even while busy with mundane tasks, or surrounded by many other people, we can still remain centred in our own quiet place and be aware of our true selves. We can remain in touch with reality.

By this I mean the reality of God in our hearts and every aspect of our lives. Keeping in touch with this reality has become increasingly difficult in western civilization, which seems to have become more and more materialistic and mind-orientated than ever before. Indeed, one of the signs of the approaching new age of Aquarius is the stimulation of humanity's mental abilities. However, it is clear that the new age is also bringing a balancing impulse—an awakening of the heart and a feeling for the interdependence of all life.

In the West there has been a great awakening of interest in eastern religions which contain precepts about this inner reality. For example, Zen Buddhism (which unites Buddhist and Taoist ways of thought and being, and became known in the West only relatively recently) teaches that true enlightenment is the recognition of both the oneness, and at the same time the uniqueness, of all forms of life. It also teaches that the universe is a single, dynamic whole.

This truth is inherent in the wisdom of the native peoples of the world—the aboriginals of Australia, of New Zealand, of Africa, of North and South America. Through the reintegration of these teachings in the West, we are seeing all over the world signs of a new sense of brotherhood, and this brotherhood embraces the world of nature and our mother earth. People are realizing again how much we lose by cutting ourselves off from our universal Mother and the help she can give us in reconnecting with the true source of our well-being and recognizing our own intuitive guidance. The wisdom of the native peoples is based upon their closeness to nature and to the great Mother of all life. For centuries now, here in our western civilization we have denied the feminine aspect of our being and thus shut ourselves off from our intuitive wisdom. We have subjugated women and plundered and misused our mother earth. Yet all of this can, and it seems *will* change, and as we step-by-step recognize women's rights and acknowledge their gifts; as we learn again by degrees how to love and respect the great Mother of all life, so also we put ourselves back into touch with God, our true spiritual selves and our intuition. A book that was once given to me entitled THE SACRED MOUNTAIN* describes how to manage your own 'vision quest' in the native American manner. In it I found these words, so much in tune with White Eagle's teaching:

Too many of us have been taught from an early age to denigrate or ignore our inner voice, the voice through which plants and animals speak to us. We have been led to doubt what we cannot directly sense or prove with our measuring sticks. We have 'learned' to devalue the inner coherency of our own self-perception of truth and meaning, preferring to put our trust in what we mistakenly believe to be the 'evidence' of our materialistic senses. If our inner voice speaks, we are skeptical of its motives and origin, seeing as how the voice apparently is attached to our mortal selves. We have 'learned' to underestimate the capacity of our minds and

*By Steven Foster and Meredith Little. Rites of Passage Press, Big Pine, California, 1984 (p. 41)

23

bodies to perceive, create and know.

We are far more than we think we are. The spirit of all things dwells within us. We can hear what the wind says to us. If you are not already convinced of this, put it to the test. Ask the wind a question about your own destiny. *If you hold your attention steadily on the subject*, the wind will answer. Then you must be willing to accept the answer, even if it seems inconsequential, or 'what I already know'. The God you worship is not apt to speak to you, or to anyone, with radiant lights or cosmic swoons. Like the voice of the Hebrew Jehovah, Truth speaks in 'a still, small voice'. Truth is very often what the little voice inside has been telling you all the while. That is why you can hear what the wind says—even if your ears are stuffed with cotton.

The exercise of intuitive cognition—one of humankind's greatest gifts—begins with the exercise of respecting and listening to your inner voice. If you cannot value your own inherent wisdom, brother Hawk, screaming above your head, has no words for you, and sweet sister Sage, upon which you pillow your dreaming head, has nothing to reveal.

For me, this passage links with some beautiful words which a friend and member of the White Eagle Lodge wrote in the last few weeks of her life:

> The voice of the wind said 'I am God',
> Breathe in my breath.
> The voice of the wind said 'I am God',
> Feel my touch on your head.
> The voice of the wind said 'I am God',
> See how I move the waves and the trees.
> The voice of the wind said 'You are a part of Me—
>   And I am God'.

And then I realized how White Eagle's teaching helps us get back into touch with our instinctive nature, our inner wisdom and the wisdom of the ancient brotherhoods and native peoples, whose lives were so different from our modern civilizations. He says, in SUN-MEN OF THE AMERICAS:

> The brothers in those days were taught consciously to inhale the light and life force in the air; to meditate on nature, on the beauty of the grass and the corn and the flowers and the trees and all the blessings of nature. And also they were taught that when they went to rest at night their last thoughts should be of God and of the attributes of God; they should open their souls to God's love, God's wisdom, God's power; to the beauty of the brotherhood of all life....
>
> In your meditation try to realize that you are not separate but that you are all of the one spirit. You have to learn that humanity is one vast brotherhood of life; that all nature is part of you—you are part of nature; you are part of the animal kingdom; you are part of the air and the birds in the air and the fish in the sea; you are part of the whole of creation, because you are a part of God and all creation is God.

All these passages give us a beautiful insight into a way in which we can become more 'constant in God', through our growing awareness of God in all nature and indeed in all life. God is in every cell of our body and in every cell of creation. Looked at in this way, it becomes surprising that we don't feel God more often, rather than marvelling when we do! Maybe we all do have more of a sense of God than we realize, but we do not put the label of 'God' on our intuitive response. We are so used to living in our heads, that we are not finely attuned to our body's wisdom, and we are always ready to doubt it anyway.

Can we do anything about this? My answer is, yes, we can.

White Eagle's teaching is intended to help us develop the inner wisdom and so here, taken from his teaching, are some of my thoughts about ways to encourage our inner awareness to grow stronger.

HOW TO ENCOURAGE AWARENESS OF OUR INNER WISDOM AND OF DIVINE GUIDANCE IN EVERYDAY LIFE

1. Stop and Listen

I believe the first thing we need to do is obvious, but often overlooked. We need to stop everything else and listen. If we take time out to do this in quiet moments, then it becomes much easier to remain aware in the midst of activity, or at a time of crisis. So, on a regular basis, take ten minutes out for *you*. Bolt your door, unplug your telephone, actually or metaphorically, and sit quietly in your own place of peace. If you can create your own simple physical sanctuary it will aid you in finding your *inner* sanctuary. The physical space can be merely a quiet corner, with a small shelf, or a table covered with a white cloth on which you place a simple lamp or candle, and maybe flowers or some object or symbol of special significance to you.

Alternatively, make your quiet space out of doors, where your communion with nature can aid your inner wisdom to reveal itself more clearly.

2. Ask

In this quiet space—think of it as a place just for you—begin quietly to watch your breathing, gradually letting it settle down into its own steady rhythm, a rhythm which is in harmony with God's rhythm in all life, with the heartbeat of our great Mother, the heartbeat of our beautiful planet earth.

Then, ask for guidance. It really helps to ask! Ask to be shown the true way, to be given a clear indication; or ask that you may be aware of your teacher. Ask your teacher to help you draw aside the veil which masks your light. 'You only have to ask in simple trust, and you shall receive' (p. 11).

3. Trust

Next try to trust that you *will* see or hear the guidance. Let yourself out of your prison. Maybe you can tell that little voice which says 'I'm never aware of anything!', 'I never see or feel my teacher', or 'I'm not that sort of person', to be quiet, and *affirm* from the Christ within you that you *are* that sort of person and that you *can* become aware of your inner guidance, maybe in the form of your teacher's voice, in the voice of the wind or of 'brother Hawk', or in a quiet inner knowing.

I had a clear demonstration of the necessity to trust that I really could see and feel, when I had my first tentative contact with my grandmother shortly after her passing in 1979. I was walking in the garden at New Lands, so happy to see it looking lovely after a time when, owing to illness, the gardener had not been able to keep it as well as usual. I felt so joyous that I literally danced across the lawn and sat on the seat at the far end. Suddenly I was aware of someone else dancing over and coming to sit beside me. I had a feeling it was my grandmother and I turned to the person I saw and said, 'Oh Nanna' (my childhood name for her). Immediately she became a little clearer to my everyday con- sciousness. The more I believed it really was her, the clearer she became, and I felt her warm hand take mine. I could see that she was now in a young body, with long dark hair. She said, 'Don't call me that. I am your sister, Minesta. I shall always be with you.' I have indeed felt her many times since then, but she has become more and more real the more I have trusted that I can see her, and that it really is her.

SIGNPOSTS THAT OUR GUIDANCE IS RIGHT

There are usually internal signposts that help reassure us we are responding to true inner guidance, but here again it really helps if we can be alert enough to notice the signs and not keep our eyes blinkered by fear or fixed ways of thinking.

1. You feel a surge of inner joy and delight and an increasing happiness in the rightness of the guidance. (Alternatively—if it is *not* right—you feel 'deadness' and discomfort inside.)

2. Things start to happen. Following that first trusting step, other things start to happen which encourage and help you open your awareness further. Things start to flow, and new doors open. Windows in your awareness are suddenly there, flung open to the glorious Sunshine, and you find that more and more you *can* hear and feel God's guidance in your life in many different ways.

3. Freedom from burden. As you increase your trust in your inner wisdom, you feel lighter and as though a heavy burden has fallen away. You are no longer so concerned about what others might think about you or what you are doing. You feel free and light-hearted. Your energies are more able to flow freely, joyously and spontaneously with the energy of the moment (which may be quite different from what you had planned or expected).

4. Confidence. New confidence floods your whole being and you are aware of being truly strong. You feel filled with love for everyone. You know that with the power of God in your heart and His love supporting you, you can truly *do anything.*

SOME FURTHER ADVICE FROM WHITE EAGLE

In the third volume in the SPIRITUAL UNFOLDMENT series White Eagle gives us clear guidance on developing inner wisdom. He says:

We suggest that you spend some time each day trying to recognize and quietly lay aside the various outer layers, the physical, astral, mental and emotional, until you find this real 'I', the eternal self.

On the one hand are all the worries, the fears, the angers, the foolishnesses, the desires—all these are the 'not I'. On the other, 'I' stands poised, polarized, still ... the spirit, the light within.

Give the 'I' every opportunity in this daily meditation to become stronger, a polarized light ... and understand that the 'I' that you identify in meditation is the real you—a God in embryo. It will never lead you off the path, never lead you astray....

The sorrows, the responsibilities, the anxieties which you think are yours, do not belong to you at all. *You* are that shining self, that light, that essence of being that you find in the hours of meditation.

THE SIX-POINTED STAR (1)

Let your spirit so shine before men that they may see their Christ in you. (p. 14)

The powerful symbol of the six-pointed star, also the symbol of the new age of Aquarius, is very significant in all the White Eagle work. It has many meanings, and at this point in each chapter I shall link its symbolism to the theme, in this case, 'the master soul is constant'.

 The upward-pointing triangle, which is one part of the star, symbolizes the little self, making an effort to open its awareness to its true self, to God (by whatever name, in whatever form), or to all that is good and true and beautiful. Any act of aspiration, or simply following the promptings of love and goodness, helps the inner light to arise, and shine more brightly.

 The downward-pointing triangle symbolizes the higher self, the true, shining, spiritual self, and also the Christ light itself, the inner master. When the little self makes the effort to rise, in a magical and spontaneous way the link with the true self is made stronger and the love and light of the spirit floods into the everyday personality.

 The two triangles united, with no divisions, symbolize our innate wholeness; the body, soul and spirit united. The star portrays the everyday self, totally illumined by the Christ-self. This is a symbol of the master soul, but also the possibility for every man and woman irrespective of colour, class or creed. It shows the illumination and transformation of the everyday human life, into a life of wholeness and happiness.

A MEDITATION ON 'THE
MASTER SOUL IS CONSTANT'

*In your meditation try to realize that you are not separate but
that you are all of the one spirit.... Humanity is one vast
brotherhood of life ... all nature is part of you ... you are part
of the animal kingdom; you are part of the air and the birds
in the air and the fish in the sea; you are part of the whole of
creation, because you are a part of God and all creation is God.*

Focus on these words of White Eagle's from SUN-MEN OF THE
AMERICAS and open your heart to your oneness with all life.
Imagine you are lying flat on the earth and breathing in harmony
with the earth. Mother earth enfolds and nurtures you. You are
one with her ... and you feel her heartbeat in everything. Her
heartbeat is the heartbeat of the angels; you are one with the
angelic and devic kingdoms. Hers is the heartbeat of the flowers;
you are one with the flowers and trees and all nature. Hers is the
heartbeat of the animals ... of the insects, the birds, the sea
creatures, the sea itself ... you are one with the waves as they lap
gently on the shore; you are one with the breeze as it softly stirs
your hair; you are one with the sun and its rays shine upon you....
The light gently wraps around you and brings a feeling of deep
security and peace. Rest in this peace....

Now turn your attention to the centre of your being, your
heart, where burns the flame of God. Here in this still centre is
the answer to all your need; here is all wisdom, all peace, all
strength, all love. Here is God. Pray that you will have the
courage, clarity and constancy to respond at all times to the

guidance of this radiant presence which will never ever leave you and never lead you astray.

AFFIRMATIONS (1)

Affirmations are short, positive statements which, when often repeated, can have a profound effect at both the conscious and unconscious levels. There are two types of affirmation:

 Those which work on mundane issues, or the little, everyday personality and its beliefs.

 The deeply spiritual affirmations which call on the Christ-self (both the higher self and the Christ in our hearts) to arise and illumine the little everyday self.

Together they can be symbolically linked to the six-pointed star symbol:

 Using both types of affirmation in combination means that we are working from both parts of the self to open up the channel and allow the shining Christ qualities which are inherent in us all to flood our whole being.

Affirmations are especially helpful when used in conjunction with prayers and meditations, but they can also be used on their own at any time of the day or night. I have found it better not to use too many different ones at once: I suggest that you choose those that seem particularly meaningful for you (maybe two or three), and keep using them for a while before you change them.

I have deliberately made a wide choice, and it may be the very phrasing that makes one appeal to you more than another.

If an affirmation is really working it may produce some resistance. That is, you may find yourself saying things like 'that isn't true', or 'that isn't me'. You may have great reluctance in saying the particular words; you may keep on forgetting the affirmation itself, or you may even find yourself getting angry about it! When there is a strong response to an affirmation, either positive or negative, it usually means it is stirring up something which is there to be looked at afresh. Try not to give up if you meet this resistance, but look on it as a sign that you are on the right track, and working with an affirmation which is really significant for you.

Choose whichever of these affirmations feels right for you at this time. Affirm:

I am constant
Divine light shines ever in my heart
I am in God and God is in me
I am one with the infinite Sun
I am one with all life
I am one with mother earth and all nature
I am one with my animal brethren
I am one with the angels
My true self is a shining spirit
I can hear the voice of my master. I can feel my inner wisdom
I know I can trust my intuition.

2

THE MASTER SOUL IS
GENTLE, LOVING, KIND

Love is the great solvent of all difficulties, all problems, all misunderstandings. Apply love, by your inner attitude towards any human problem.

MANY OF the great saints and mystics of all religious paths are known for their ability to remain steadfastly loving in the face of great adversity. The stories of Jesus's life show the depth of his compassion and ability to love and to forgive, perhaps the most remarkable of all being his forgiveness of Judas, and his words of general forgiveness while hanging on the cross. In our present day the Dalai Lama is for me a supreme example of love and forgiveness in the face of terrible persecution; another modern-day 'saint' is Mother Teresa, who has found so much inspiration for her work in following Jesus's example. We are told that when she is asked how she keeps going with her work, she replies that she sees Christ in even the sickest and saddest among her patients.

A basic keynote of all White Eagle's teaching is love, and many people have been drawn to his work because they feel at home with this vibration. His words give us a beautiful vision of love.

He tells us that true love is not emotionalism, which sweeps us off our feet, for 'love divorced from wisdom is no longer love', but rather, the giving of 'the highest and truest within you to your brother' (pp. 24-25). However much we are inspired by words like these, we may still feel that when it comes down to practical day-to-day relationships, they are extremely hard to live up to. I found it very helpful when someone told me, 'If it is difficult for me to love someone, I remember "we all share the same heartbeat".'

Sometimes our inability to feel what we think of as 'enough' love may stem from emotional overloading. For example, if your daily work involves nursing or caring and you also have a family or many friends in need of emotional support, you may become so drained with giving all the time, that in the end your system becomes exhausted. The answer to this is to make sure you arrange enough space in your life to give time and recreation to your own self, which also has needs and cannot cope forever with the denial of them. In our anxiety to follow a spiritual path and be of service to others, we can often take on unnecessary burdens and try to do too much for others. Many of us have been brought up with injunctions such as 'don't be selfish', and in fact taught to feel that it is wrong to look at our own needs. Yet the denial of our own needs ultimately defeats itself; it is a violence towards ourselves, just as much as the denial of others' needs is violence. Eventually, through such denial, we find ourselves emotionally empty, hurt and deeply resentful inside.

Here is a story I like very much: a teacher was walking in the woods one day when he came upon a man who was feverishly trying to cut wood with a saw. He looked exhausted and so the teacher said, 'Why don't you take a break for a few minutes and sharpen your saw?' The man refused, saying, 'I'm too busy.

There's too much to do. I can't possibly stop sawing!'.

I can certainly relate to this story. I know how often I have felt it impossible to take a break because 'there's so much to do!' But, of course, what happens if we never take time to 'sharpen our saw' is that it becomes increasingly inefficient, until eventually it is useless. The same happens to our poor body, mind and emotions, if they are never given rest and recreation.

However, if we do just this—stop, and take time to 'sharpen our saw'—we can return to our work with new strength and delight. (I certainly found this recently, after I took a sabbatical from my own work.) If we do give ourselves love and plenty of time for refreshment, we can reconnect much more easily with the inexhaustible well of love. Affirmations (such as *I am divine love*, or *I am enfolded in the love of divine Mother*) help in this. I have also found it helpful to take time out to walk quietly on mother earth—in any beautiful place, on land or by the sea. As I walk, sometimes I consciously breathe up through my feet the nurturing love of divine Mother and feel it flow up through my whole body and fill my heart. If you like gardening, you may find great inner refreshment and re-creation through the contact of your hands and feet with the earth and plants. I remember that my grandmother liked to spend time in her garden like this.

White Eagle reminds us that the true source of love is not found outside ourselves; it is found deep within the heart of each one of us; it is the God within. Here in this secret sanctuary is the answer to all our needs. It is significant, I think, that Jesus's celebrated words about 'loving thy neighbour as thyself' follow on from 'love of the Lord thy God', for the greater our awareness of God's love, the more clearly we can mirror this love in our own lives and in all our relationships.

Loving is an act of both giving and receiving, yet when it

comes to accepting love in our own lives we are often more at sea than we realize! For instance, we may make the mistake of demanding of life that love come from outside of ourselves, that is, we want another to love us, or to find love in a predefined way, not recognizing that the love we receive is a mirror of the love we allow ourselves within. Then, when the person or happening we are looking to for fulfilment does not live up to our hopes, we feel let down. Sometimes this looking outside ourselves leads us to behave unwisely in relationships. For example, it might lead us into over-indulgence: 'If I give him everything, he must love me'; or over-possessiveness: 'If I hold on really tightly and make life so uncomfortable for her if she does not do what I want, she will have to stay with me'. In other circumstances, our need to feel successful and secure in the world may lead us to push our children to succeed where we have 'failed'.

I have made both these mistakes in my own relationships with those I love. At one time I fell so desperately in love, and my whole happiness seemed to depend on my love being recipro-cated, that I felt I would do anything to gain and then keep that love just for me. Eventually I learnt that emotional dependence never fills that empty space inside and only leads to a deeper insecurity and an emotional seesaw between delight and despair. Then, with my children, I made the mistake of trying to make up for things I felt I had missed in my own childhood by pushing them to do those very things themselves. In my anxiety to give them opportunities I had not had, I did not stop to consider what they themselves actually wanted to do. To give one example, I had longed to be a Girl Guide and was never able to attend Guide meetings (although I did become a 'Lone Guide'). Consequently, I was so thrilled when Sara became a Guide that I pushed her to work for lots of badges and take part in everything.

Unfortunately, she was not really enjoying it, and such was the underlying emotional pressure I was putting on her and the unconscious manipulation (on the lines of, 'If you really love me, you will do this for me') that it was a long time before she could pluck up the courage to tell me she wanted to give Guides up. When she did finally do so, I was very upset and tried to persuade her to continue. It was only some years later that I realized what I had been doing. Trying to manipulate our loved ones (and we often do it unconsciously) or holding on, never leads to happiness in the end.

A feeling of inner security is a first step in all these problems. We seek to manipulate and control when we are feeling insecure, empty or unloved in our little selves. The only true and eternal security lies in God. Security comes from knowing that 'underneath are the everlasting arms', and that our lives are held in the care of One who knows our need even better than we do ourselves. The more secure the little self is, the easier it is to respond in truly loving ways to all life's situations, and to set our loved ones free to follow their own inner light and choose paths which are uniquely right for *them*.

DIFFERENT KINDS OF LOVE

We have all chosen different personalities for what we need to learn in this lifetime. It is not given to every one of us to be extrovert, the 'life and soul of the party'; not all of us want to be effusive in our demonstration of love for others. Yet everyone would agree that that doesn't mean we don't love them. Love takes many forms and all forms of loving are ways into loving more completely. All forms manifest the divine love in some way. It is just as loving to be still and peaceful, and listen to another with full attention, or to visualize someone in healing light when they are in need, as it is to articulate our love all the time. It is at least as loving to give others their freedom (an acknowledgment of the unique expression of their true self), and to be undemanding, as it is always to be concerned for their daily or emotional needs. There are relationship situations where the other person's extreme concern is just too much. I can recall times in my own life when, far from feeling supported by this sort of love, I have felt trapped and drained by it. By contrast, the friend who said, 'I am always there if you need me', gave me loving support of a kind which also set me free.

We all need to know that no matter how different we are, we are capable of loving in our own unique ways, and all expressions of love are creative, progressive and uplifting. Little acts of kindness and thoughtfulness can be just as much an expression of divine love working through human life as great acts of sacrifice. Indeed, small things can make all the difference at the end (or in the middle) of a long hard day—the bunch of flowers, the loving note, the welcome cup of tea, the washing-up all done, the ironing finished without any asking, the unexpected little treat or gift, the warm hug and simple 'I really love you, darling'. They are all expressions of real loving which we can give one another—if only we stop and think to open our eyes to our brother's or sister's true need.

So much seeming thoughtlessness and lack of love is the result of not opening our eyes, and being too busy with our own preoccupations to notice other people. In recent years I have been blessed with two secretaries in succession who have supported me in every way and have been very efficient at their jobs too, but something I have particularly appreciated is their thought-fulness and their remembrance of what is going on in my life. Although they have not been involved in the spiritual activities of the White Eagle Lodge, I have always been touched when, as so often, they have asked me the day after a big service or function, 'How did it go?'. Neither was too busy or too full up with her own concerns to remember.

Someone else who will always live in my memory as one of the most loving and thoughtful people I have ever known is my father. It was never too much trouble for him to perform some act of kindness. He was always thinking ahead and planning things to smooth the way of others. This caring always came first for him. He would always have extra food in stock, in case anyone else should need something, and a funny card ready, to produce a smile on someone's birthday. Many, many patients in the White Eagle Lodge were cheered by his humorous little drawings in 'get-well' cards, and his kind and thoughtful comments. He was writing these notes to patients the day he died, and many have said how he continues to reassure them even now, as he seems to have a particular knack of making people aware of his smiling, cheerful presence in his new body of light.

GENTLENESS

So many of us feel unable, at times, to be gentle. We may feel that it is not given to everyone to be gentle: that some are gentle, and others are dynamic and incisive. Yet gentleness is something we all can feel, if we are prepared to feel vulnerable too (and it doesn't mean we can't be dynamic as well!). This ties in with what I have already said about loving—we can exhibit gentleness when we feel *safe*. Sometimes we may feel gentle inside, yet behave aggressively because we feel insecure or under attack in some way. Yet an animal will lie down with its most vulnerable parts exposed in order to stop a continuing fight. We could learn from our 'lesser' brethren in this. Even when we are seemingly under attack, softness or gentleness towards the other person will often help to defuse the situation. Jesus was gentle, even when scourged and abused. There are many stories of eastern teachers reacting peacefully and lovingly when confronted with ignorance and insult. I particularly love the story of Hakuin (a Zen master) who was falsely accused of seducing a village girl and being the father of her child. When confronted by her parents he merely replied, 'Is that so?'. He provided for the girl and her baby and was not at all troubled that he had lost his reputation of being a pure and holy man. Later, when the girl told the truth, and the parents apologized to Hakuin, all he said again was 'Is that so?'. We are all so apt to feel we have to defend ourselves, and yet, as this story beautifully illustrates, a master feels no such need, and reacts with loving kindness and gentleness at all times.*

REMAINING LOVING UNDER STRESS

Here are some ideas—indeed an emergency programme—for relationship problems and when you are feeling hurt or angry, confused or hopeless.

First, a key phrase to memorize:
Stop and remember: let go and listen.
Stop everything else and give yourself time to use this formula.

STOP

Remember: there *is* something you can do; you are not powerless; the star (which represents the Christ you) has the power to work miracles.

REMEMBER

*This story, and subsequent ones on a Zen theme, are from the book ZEN FOR BEGINNERS by Judith Blackstone and Zoran Josipovic (Unwin Paperbacks, London, 1986), to whom I am greatly indebted.

LET GO

Stop holding tightly onto the problem, or the feeling. Let go, lay down your problems, and surrender your little self's desire for things to work out in a particular way, or for the other person to behave as you want them to or think they 'should'.

STEP ASIDE

Recognize it is only a little part of the *real you* which is feeling the hurt, anger or confusion. Say: 'Yes, it is there.' Acknowledge the feeling (it doesn't help to pretend it isn't there!). Feel it. But remember, 'This is not *me*. I'm not that feeling. That's just my little self, learning lessons through that feeling.'

EMER-GENCY LOVE

Give your hurting self an emergency dose of warm, 'motherly' love and reassurance. One way to do this is to picture your little self actually *as* a small child and see it going to mother for comfort. Let yourself be the mother. Don't push your 'child' away and tell it off. Give it the love it needs. Then, you will have the emotional calm and confidence to take the next steps.

THINK OF YOUR MASTER

If you find it helpful, think of a master or your teacher. Ask yourself:
—How would he/she react?
—How would he/she have you react?
—Picture him/her standing before you and open your heart to his/her great love.

WAIT AND LISTEN

Wait and listen. As you train yourself to become very peaceful and still in body, mind and emotions, you will find yourself more and more able to feel love and react in a loving way.

The 'waiting and listening' may also require *doing* on

43

the outer planes. A significant part of real loving is being able to stand back and truly listen to the other person.

ALLOW

Allow God's love to flow through your heart, your gentle touch, your kind words, or your wise understanding.

FORGIVE

Allow God's love to lift you into that higher place where your perspective is clear and true, and you can truly forgive both little selves. White Eagle says:

> When you come up against personal hurts try to attune yourself to the heights.... Think of the one with whom you are at variance and a shaft of Light will go to him and there will be a change in the position and all will go smoothly. Thus are crooked places made straight. (p. 26)

ACTION

From the clear perspective of your true self you will receive the guidance you need about any practical action which is necessary for healing and enabling for everyone in their growth.

Here's a postscript from Anna, my colleague and friend who has helped me so much in recent years in my personal journey, and in the writing of this book:

'I can state that quite without exception, when I have had the courage to look up to God and ask for help in a crisis of feeling, the help has *always* come. What is difficult is *remembering* it at the time when one is feeling so bad.'

THE SIX-POINTED STAR (2)

When you come up against personal hurts try to attune yourself to the heights. (p. 26)

 The upward-pointing triangle symbolizes the awakening of the little self to truly loving, through:

—reconnecting with the source of love and light which is already there in our hearts.

—stopping identifying our whole self with the 'little self'.

—the recognition of what is getting in the way, such as the little self's hurt reactions.

—the recognition of the lessons the little self is needing to learn, which is why the higher shining self is setting up these particular tests and problems.

—reconnecting with God's love which is always there in our hearts.

 The downward-pointing triangle symbolizes God's total love for us, our teacher's love and our true self. When the little self looks up, it reconnects itself with God's love and the illumination of the true self, so the inner guidance can flow freely, ever supporting us in our growing.

 The star symbolizes becoming totally illumined by God's love. This true and unconditional love transforms all our relationships....

A MEDITATION ON 'THE MASTER SOUL IS GENTLE, LOVING, KIND'

Love is an inward beauty which flows from the heart, from the life. (p. 27)

Create a beautiful garden in your imagination and picture yourself sitting there, surrounded by peace and beauty. Open all your inner senses to make it even more real.... Smell the fragrant blossom, listen to the bird-song and the rustle of the little animals, feel the soft grass and watch the nature spirits at work and play in the flowers.

Now open your heart to the great love which is enfolding all this life and you ... the love of Father–Mother God. This love embraces all life and helps you feel love for life in all its diversity. Here in this heavenly garden it is easy to feel this love, and particularly the nurturing love of the Mother-principle of God. You may even 'see' Her in the form of a beautiful woman; but open your heart particularly to the intuitive, enfolding influence which wraps around you like a gentle cloak. As you nestle in this soft velvety cloak, you have a feeling of absolute safety and security ... you feel the quickening of divine love in your heart. Feel it as a little flame within your heart, the Christ child in you. Nurture your Christ flame, as it nestles in the security of your inner being. Feel it grow strong and bright so that it can shine forth in a radiant light and inspire your actions with thoughtfulness and gentle, loving kindness.

AFFIRMATIONS (2)

Choose whichever of these affirmations feels right for you at this time.

I am gentle, loving and kind
I am secure in the love of my Father–Mother God
Divine Mother nurtures and enfolds me
I can love everyone unconditionally, including myself
I love life in all its diversity
I love all creation
I am divine love.

3

THE MASTER SOUL IS TOLERANT

Withhold judgment and criticism. The human way is to judge in haste the actions of others. But the divine way is to remain quiet and loving. You are divine as well as human and you are here on earth to learn to manifest divinity.

MANY OF the international and religious conflicts we are experiencing in our world today are the result of entrenched attitudes and the inability to understand other ways of looking at life. A master's understanding is broad and wide and embraces every different attitude. He or she would never say that a belief is the only right one and therefore all others are wrong. A master soul radiates love towards all life and tolerance towards all the many ways of being which make up human life. As the third Patriarch of Zen, Seng-ts'an, said: 'The Great Way is very simple; just avoid picking and choosing.' I believe that tolerance is one of the most beautiful qualities which we can strive to manifest in our own relationships and in our attitude towards life. In my personal times of contemplation I often think of the founders of the great world religions, and particularly at the present moment, Jesus and Mohammed, and feel they are working quietly on the inner planes to radiate greater tolerance and understanding in the hearts of their ardent followers.

Fanatically-held views can lead to great tension and conflict. Wisdom is yielding and flexible; as I say in a later chapter, it flows gently like a great river. It changes its outer form to suit the circumstances of the moment and it never becomes rigid.

In recent years I have done a lot of travelling, and one of the things I have been learning from this is a more tolerant attitude. I was in Turkey once at the time of their Bayram celebrations. Bayram is as important to the Turks as Christmas is to those in a Christian culture, but the focal point of their festival involves the public killing, for every household, of a sheep. Muslims are very sincere in their belief that this is right and holy, and it is done in remembrance of the biblical story of Abraham and Isaac. So great was Abraham's love of God and his acceptance of His will, that he was prepared to sacrifice to God that which he loved most in all the world—his first-born son, Isaac. At the very last moment Isaac was reprieved, for a sheep appeared and God told him to kill that instead. So the killing is done in remembrance of a Muslim's absolute one-pointed dedication to following God's will. The very word 'Islam' means 'submission'—to the will of Allah.

However, I was extremely distressed about this remembrance done in the form of killing animals—even though animals are killed just as much in the West, and the killing of the sheep didn't seem too remote from the tradition of the Christmas turkey. On the morning the killing was actually happening I walked alone by the sea and was thinking about how terrible it was, and how misguided the people must be to believe that God actually wanted them to kill these poor animals, when I had an experience which I know I shall remember all my life. Suddenly, in my inner vision, I saw a being of light coming towards me, resolving itself out of the sunlight as it shone on the water, and I felt a great ray of love and compassionate understanding enfold me.

Then I heard the words, 'Jenny, you are learning tolerance', and I realized how intolerant my thoughts had been. I saw how much I needed to let go of my conviction that I was right and that these people were wrong. Tolerance is an attitude towards *people* and though I retained an abhorrence of the action I saw how easy it is to fall into the trap of thinking that one's own belief system is the only correct one. On reflection, I have realized that the loving, tolerant reaction is to see all concerned in the light and to try letting go all harsh critical thought, offering everything to the wisdom of God's love. There is so much we do not yet understand, from our earthly perspective, about the seeming complexity of life—for example, how much Muslims may be learning through their devotion to Allah and His will, which is such an inherent part of their religion. Also, we ourselves need forgiveness for our own cruelty and lack of understanding. We may not kill animals ourselves, but there are many ways in which some of us still collude in their deaths or cruel treatment.

All thoughts of antagonism create a negative vibration which in itself helps to perpetuate cruelty through increasing the negative energy. What is needed is a stimulation of the light within us—that is to say, positive, loving thought—so that in God's great wisdom He can bring about transformation in the most loving and appropriate ways.

In seeking to develop the quality of tolerance within ourselves, I find it is helpful to think often of everyone's uniqueness: every person is a unique, creative part of God. If this is so, then every expression of the truth has to be relative. The only conscience is within each person's own heart and their own relationship with

God, and no-one else can challenge this. All we can do is follow our own inner light as closely as we can.

If we do hold very rigid views it may well be that circumstances come into our lives which force us to see another point of view. White Eagle teaches that this is one of the divine laws which govern life; if we swing very radically in one direction, the pendulum is bound to swing back the other way at some time, until eventually the point of perfect balance is maintained.

I have an amusing little story on this theme. One of my daughter's university friends had been a fanatical vegan for some years and was very intolerant of people who ate meat and even of those who ate dairy products. Suddenly she fell in love with a young man who turned out to be a butcher, and found herself going out on dates in a van with carcasses hanging in the back. Her love provided a catalyst which helped her open her heart to a little more tolerance.

It is worth recollecting the story of Gautama Buddha, who had firsthand experience, before his enlightenment, of the two extremes: great material wealth and indulgence, and harsh denial. After his enlightenment he advocated 'the middle way' as the best path to follow. In human relationships we often need to relax preconceived ideas about what is 'right' or 'wrong', or the particular way things 'should' be done. Difficulty arises when two people feel so differently about something that there is a conflict about how to proceed. This is where there is the need to compromise. It does not mean we have to go against the inner promptings of our heart, but we need constantly to ask to be wise enough to know what really is the heart's prompting, and what is the emotional self's, as well as when to speak and when to keep silent. So often we feel that for harmony to exist everyone must feel the same way, or be the same, as us: and yet a great feeling of rightness comes to us when we can love someone for being true to their own heart, although their truth may be different from ours, or may even cause us pain. If two people can do this for each other, it actually brings unity between them and a true feeling of brotherhood.

One of the most beautiful things about the love of a master is that it is a love which just *is*. It is not a love which is conditional upon anything. It is a wonderful security—indeed, perhaps the greatest security—to know this. We need never feel that we have to do something or be something for God or our teacher to love us. You may think, 'But surely, God, or my teacher, will love me more if I am good and work very hard for the Light?'. I believe God loves us totally and unconditionally. Even at the human level, it is normal for parents to love their children even when they believe they have been naughty; and God is surely a perfect parent to us.

Our teacher loves in this way, too, for he or she is one who can truly reflect God's love in a human way. White Eagle has said elsewhere, 'True brotherhood is to be able to identify with both saint and murderer.' In our true selves it is not so hard to mirror this beautiful loving acceptance of human nature and human freewill, but in our little selves it may take many lifetimes of persistence. White Eagle encourages us in all our efforts to view life from a broader perspective, and to help our everyday little self to let go of feelings of criticism and judgment, and replace these with love.

THE LAW OF CAUSE AND EFFECT IN ACTION

If our behaviour does not affect God's or our teacher's love for us, you may wonder what effect it does have? It must have *some* effect? Yes, of course, White Eagle would say, for the law of cause and effect—as you sow, so you reap—is always operating, and our behaviour comes back to us like a boomerang. In a teaching in our magazine STELLA POLARIS, he says:

> Some day you will see how your every act, word, and even thought sends out its ripples, its vibrations like a stone cast into the water. As you give, so you will receive. The breaking of divine law used to be called sinful. People ask today what is all this talk about sin, this out-of-date jargon? No; sin is the breaking of the one supreme law of brotherhood, of love. You read in your Bible: *'Am I my brother's keeper?'* Yes, everyone is his brother's keeper!... Every one of us is responsible for our thoughts, words and actions. When in spirit you are somehow able to see what harm man's careless, thoughtless actions and words (maybe your own) have done to some fellow creature, you will long to put things right. People who carelessly say reincarnation is false do much harm; because the soul, once it sees the error of its ways, longs beyond all else to put its sins right.

How we are in the world outside is really a reflection of how we are to ourselves. So, if we are intolerant of ourselves and others, we will experience conditions of intolerance that eventually enable us to see our intolerance within. White Eagle teaches us that our thoughts create karma just as do our actions. He tells us that when we pass on to the spirit life, we find ourselves in a world created not just by our past actions, but also very much by our thoughts. However, it is not just the next life which is subject to this law: it operates in our life here and now, too. We would be wise not to dwell too much on negative thoughts of any kind, about others or about ourselves. If we are constantly thinking judgmentally, these thoughts will come back to us in some way. White Eagle says:

> Often you see only the rough exterior of a man or woman.
> If only you could cut away the thorns, you would find a gentle
> and beautiful nature beneath, sleeping. Strive always to find
> the princess hidden behind all prickly growths. (pp. 33–34)

We all possess the light within; we all have that higher, that 'princess' self. We should therefore deal with each other lovingly, always seeking the best, and encouraging beauty in every possible way. If you feel all too aware of the 'prickly growths', as White Eagle calls them, in your little self, try, as I have said, to look on that little self exactly as you would a child who, though it needs to learn wisdom, needs lots of love and forgiveness too.

GUILT

1. Guilt about failure or 'not being good enough'

Guilt is one of the things which lead us into negative thought-patterns and make it more difficult for us to practise what White Eagle is teaching.

I think most people feel guilty at times, but maybe it becomes even more of a problem if we are consciously following a spiritual path. Fear that we shall fail or are basically 'not good enough' can lead to an even greater tendency to chastise ourselves. We may have a set idea of what we should be like in order to 'be a spiritual person', and whenever we fall short of this we feel bad about ourselves. But in actual fact I think that what 'being a spiritual person' really means is different for everyone, because we are all unique. There is no one set pattern or formula to which everyone has to conform in order to be 'spiritual'. When reading through my first draft for this chapter, my editor, Colum Hayward, gave me his definition. It really feels 'right' for me, so I would like to pass it on. He said, 'If I were writing I would want to say that "being spiritual" is what we are all the time we are in touch with our true selves. There is nothing about spirituality which is different from ordinary life.' This reminds me of the well-known Zen saying: 'Before enlightenment chop wood and carry water; after enlightenment chop wood and carry water.'

So if you find yourself feeling you are 'not spiritual enough' or feel guilty about anything, try to let go of those thoughts, which are destructive, and instead centre yourself again in your awareness of God's love. Allow this love to be your guiding light in all you say and do. In God's eyes you are always okay and always accepted, and every activity of daily life is spiritual.

2. Guilt about sexuality

One particular area which guilt regularly creeps into when we are trying to follow what we think of as a spiritual way of life is our sexuality and our feelings about our physical bodies. It is not more spiritual to deny ourselves the pleasure of life in a physical body, or endlessly to follow cleansing diets, or for that matter to engage in marathon programmes of meditation. Building great walls around our 'temple' simply conceals the beauty of the divine! Scourging ourselves will only cause an extreme reaction in the other direction at some future time. Balance is always the way. It is no more spiritual to be celibate than to enjoy the intimacy of happy, physical loving, unless celibacy is a path which the true self has chosen as the very best way forward for the growth of its understanding. Sometimes a pull towards celibacy and denial of our sexuality may be our little self's wanting to escape from the demands of a really close relationship with another human being; or it may be the result of deep programming that there is something sinful about sex. Of course, there isn't. Making love is one of God's many joyful gifts in our lives. White Eagle tells us elsewhere:

Enjoy your life. Be happy and thankful for every glorious sensation which your body rightly gives to you. Enjoy your food. Let it be clean, pure food. Enjoy your recreation. Enjoy all forms of bodily exercise. Enjoy every gift of life, but never forget the Source of your life to which you owe everything.

So don't deny yourself physical pleasure, or pleasure of any other sort, in the belief that you will therefore be more spiritual. Follow spiritual law in your relationships, including your relationship with yourself, but don't try to be holy! Just be natural and warm and loving. White Eagle tells us to be loving in everything we do, including being loving to our bodies.

When people ask me for guidance about the rights and wrongs of sexual relationships, I explain that there are three basic criteria I like to consider:

First, not to judge anyone else for what they seem to be doing. The law of brotherhood is based on tolerance and loving understanding. No-one in a physical body can possibly understand exactly how it is for someone else. A master does have a much greater understanding, and still would never judge or condemn anyone. A master's perspective is broad and long, and totally unlimited by the conditioning of a particular society's ideas of what is 'right' or 'wrong'.

Secondly, live by the law of love in your understanding of other people's relationships and of your own. 'Do unto others as you would be done by.'

Thirdly, always be guided by the wisdom of your inner light, as to what is 'right' or 'wrong' for you, but do not try to impose your ideas upon others.

A master would encourage us to follow our inner light at all times. If this meant being in an unconventional or non-traditional relationship (for example a homosexual one) he would not sit in judgment of us, nor would he want us to feel guilty or judge ourselves. The brotherhood law is always the law of love, and is there in Shakespeare's words: 'This above all: to thine own self be true, And it must follow, as the night the day, Thou can'st not then be false to any man.' White Eagle has a different view of what the Christian world has called sin. He tells us (in THE PATH OF THE SOUL):

We would say that sin is a failure to go direct to the truth. When striking out his first furrow across a field a ploughman has always to keep his eye fixed upon a distant marking-post. If his eye wanders he cannot drive a straight furrow. This applies also to our own actions, particularly to our relations with our brother men. We sin when we fail to drive a straight furrow to the marking-post. Some people may protest that they have always lived a good life, and how can they then have sinned? The answer is that every time the soul does not live truth from its innermost being, it is sinning. Some bodily sins we would not call sins at all. Sin is the failure of the soul to live truly, to express truth in thought and word and deed.

FORGIVENESS

Being able truly to forgive is another way we can express our love and tolerance. Forgiveness helps us put our guilt feelings into the past. If we can forgive, we stop being stuck in the past, introspectively submerged in recrimination or resentment. It helps us see the beauty of the present moment.

There are, of course, two aspects of forgiveness: being able to forgive someone else who has hurt us and being able to forgive ourselves.

A while ago I had an experience about forgiving and loving my little self. It happened on a day I was feeling rather despondent, and not liking myself much for feeling like this. I stood on the hilltop outside the Temple at New Lands, as I often do, and tried to 'lift myself up' enough in order to send out healing light to the world. At first it was a real problem to make any spiritual contact, and then I was suddenly aware of a great light shining down on me. Out of this light came my teacher and although at first he seemed quite far off, he gradually became very close and very human indeed. He just stood in front of me and smiled and poured love into my heart. I knew he loved everything about me, and was especially gentle and understanding with my little self, which felt so low in spirit. It was as though, beneath his gaze, my little self became a restless, unhappy child, and that he picked up the little child and cradled it to his heart. He soothed my little inner child and poured so much love into it, healing and comforting it. Then he handed it back to nestle in *my* heart, and told me to love and forgive my little child too....

'If he, who is so beautiful, so great in spirit, can love like this....', I thought. I was overcome by his shining example and inspired to keep on trying to love and forgive my little self—and others—as he loves us.

It is hard to forgive oneself, but often harder to forgive someone else. I have realized from my own experience that agreeing that to be able to forgive is right and what we need to do, is a very different matter from actually being able to do it when the matter for forgiveness goes very deep. I had been trying to forgive someone for a long time for something which had hurt me very deeply but, however hard I tried, there was still a knot of pain and resentment deep in my solar plexus. Suddenly, though, after some months of using a forgiveness meditation and affirmation, I was aware of a shift. I experienced it as an almost physical sensation of release and letting go, and I felt my heart centre opening in greater love and new understanding. Suddenly and unexpectedly the real forgiveness happened—but it was spontaneous: it came when my little self was ready, and it would not be forced to happen before this. When it comes, it truly seems like 'the grace of God'—a pure and beautiful fragrance which touches and enfolds the hurt little self. I realized that it is the little self which has the problem with forgiveness, for of course our true selves have the clear perspective of past-life karma and all the factors involved, and do not find it hard to forgive the little self of another soul. I believe there are a number of reasons why this is so.

First, there may be a feeling in the little self that if it forgives, it has given in or colluded with the other person's little self, or that it has lost face.

There may also be a feeling of wanting the other to see what they have done and how much hurt has been caused. This can lead to going around looking very miserable all the time, so the other person really can see!

Thirdly, there may be a feeling (maybe very natural and understandable!) of wanting to hit back.

If we are able to be truly honest and acknowledge that one or other of these hidden feelings is getting in the way of forgiving, we can work on that, too, and release it. It may be that the other person's action is the result of their own deep hurt, and the more we can understand this, the easier it is to let our own hurt go, and accept. Time and a wider perspective are great healers, for often we get very upset by things that do not matter so much in the long run. Sometimes it seems to take a very long time indeed to be able to forgive, but in reality we are taking the process one step at a time, like a journey. The next section is an illustration of a typical sequence which may help you to come through to a new situation.

THE FORGIVENESS JOURNEY

The little self is hurt....
1. Ask for help to let go the hurt.
2. Wait patiently for that help to come.
3. Encourage your little self with lots of love to 'keep on keeping on' (White Eagle's famous phrase, p. 29), letting go the past and moving forward into the Sunlit future.
4. Use forgiveness prayers, affirmations and visualizations.
All these steps lead up to the actual act of release which allows the grace of God to enfold and heal and bring true forgiveness. Forgiveness sets the soul free.

Finally, a friend in Australia shared with me recently the following 'forgiveness prayer' which he has found very helpful to use while on just such a journey as this:

> Mother, Father God,
> through the Divine in me,
> I forgive the human in me
> and the human in ....
> over our problem concerning ....

He says that using this prayer has helped him really let go and forgive far more quickly than hitherto. I hope it will help you, too.

THE SIX-POINTED STAR (3)

And how, you ask, are we to walk the spiritual path? We answer: say little, love much; give all; judge no man; aspire to all that is pure and good—and keep on keeping on. (p. 29)

Changing our negative thought-patterns. The upward-pointing triangle symbolizes our efforts to change our thoughts and let the negativity go which tempts us to blame, judge and criticize both others and ourselves; it symbolizes our perspective on life broadening to embrace with loving tolerance everyone else's view-point ... bringing an opening of our awareness to the fragrance of a master's love, and the breadth of his/her tolerance.

The master's love. In the symbolism of the downward-pointing triangle, a master's love and tolerance embraces all life. The fragrance of this love pours into our hearts, helping us mirror it in our lives.

A joy-filled life. The star symbolizes our illumined, joy-filled life, when we have raised ourselves and 'opened the door' to allow the light of the spirit to transform our consciousness, so that we view life from a clear perspective and feel tolerance for all.

A MEDITATION ON 'THE
MASTER SOUL IS TOLERANT'

If He who is so beautiful, so great in spirit, can continue to love you, in spite of all, is it so hard for you to give your little love to your brother man, and all living things? (p. 24)

As you sit quietly attuning yourself to the light of God, the light of the star, your teacher comes to you in spirit. He/she is the essence of divine love: look into his/her eyes and see the great love shining there; a love which is all understanding, all tolerance and acceptance. Hold out your cupped hands to receive the rose that is given to you now. Feel the softness of its delicate petals, inhale its fragrance and notice its perfect form. Then place the rose on your heart centre and absorb it into your being.

This rose is a symbol of God's love for you. Absorb this love into every cell of your being, your little self and your true self.

This love helps you let go all the things which do not matter. This love helps you forgive. This love helps you feel true love and tolerance of your own little self and of the little self of all your brethren.

This love is perfect ... and so are you.

Now imagine your little self as a tiny child. This child needs lots of tender love; pick up your child and lift it into your heart. Cradle it here in the fragrant petals of the rose, where all hurts can be healed. Your child is perfect—perfected in God's light and love, safe, secure and at peace.... Pray that all your thoughts and actions in your outer life are illumined by this tolerant, mother love which flowers deep in your heart.

AFFIRMATIONS (3)

These are my chosen affirmations on tolerance. Choose whichever feels right for you at this time.

I am tolerant and kind
I forgive myself and I let love into my life
I love and forgive .... (name)
I value my unique contribution in the brotherhood of life
I value everyone's *unique contribution to life. I am filled with
light and love*
I am perfect as my Father created me perfect
My heart is open and accepting of every way of being.

4

THE MASTER SOUL IS
CALM, QUIET AND STEADY

A Master has learned the supreme lesson of the conservation of energy; he will never waste his energy, the vital force, the God-life. He trains himself to remain calm and tranquil in spite of the storms of life.

IN MY IDEAL picture of myself I am always able to keep calm, no matter what crisis is going on around me, and this calm poise is not swept away in the turbulent tide of emotional response to difficult situations. I think we would all like to stay poised in any situation, and most people are looking for more inner peace and less stress in their lives. Usually in our search for the elusive conditions which will help us feel peaceful we are looking outside ourselves, but true peace is not really dependent on outer things at all. White Eagle's teaching in this chapter of THE QUIET MIND makes this very clear. He tells us that peace comes from God, from a clear awareness of God's light within our own being, and of our true self. It is the little self which becomes upset and harassed—not the true self. The true self sees clearly and has an innate trust in God; because of this it is at peace. Every human being has the potential to stay totally calm and at peace. A master is always centred in peace. No matter what is going on, he or she is always calm and aware of the perfection of God's plan.

You may be thinking, 'It is all very well for a master, but what about my life right now? Maybe my real self is peaceful, but it is my little self which is not. How can I help my little self? How can I feel peace *today* when my life is in disarray and I am filled with pain?' So here are some pointers which I hope may help.

LEARNING TO FLOW WITH 'HOW THINGS ARE'

One of the reasons we find it hard to be peaceful is that we can get very fixed ideas about how we want things to turn out, and about what is right and good. Then we get upset and stressed if things do not fit into this plan. Often they don't, for the experiences the true self has set up for the greatest learning and soul growth can be very different from what we think we want. The only way out of this situation which will lead to peace is to flow with 'how things are'. This is one reason a master is always peaceful—because he does not try to impose his will on God's will. Indeed, his will *is* God's will. 'Live today with God,' says White Eagle, 'and your future can hold nothing but joy' (p. 45).

Living with God means being able to flow with the universe, with the way things are moving, and trust that all things are working together for our ultimate good. This is a basic part of Taoist and Zen philosophy. There is a story of a monk who said to a master, 'Please show me the way to enlightenment.' The master responded, 'Do you hear the murmuring sound of the mountain stream?'.

When the monk replied, 'Yes, I do,' the master then said, 'Enter there.'

So much of our unhappiness is caused by our personal

resistance to, and lack of acceptance of, the way things are turning out in our lives. I went through a very unhappy period in my life when I was longing for a second child. Every month when my period came and I knew I was not pregnant, I was cast into depression and, having a tendency to impatience anyway, I did not know how I could get through the next month until there was another chance again. I can remember much distress and crying in my heart, 'Oh God, why do I have to wait so long. Why does it have to be like this?' Having been brought up with White Eagle's teaching, my brain told me it was my karma and that birth and death are subject to exact and beautiful law. But this mental knowledge, which was also within my true self, did not stop my little self hurting and rebelling against my deeper wisdom. Everywhere I looked, other people seemed to be happily pushing babies around in prams; and I could truly understand the deep and desperate longing that occasionally drives a woman to steal someone else's baby from a pram. Then one day, magic seemed to have happened and the doctor confirmed that I was pregnant. But worse was to come, for just a few weeks later I had a miscarriage. It took me many days to regain my inner peace, and trust again in God and the perfection of His timing.

I now acknowledge that our set ideas about how we want things to be can be like banging against a locked door—all that happens is we get exhausted and bruised, just as I did when I was longing for another baby *now*! Maybe all the time there is another door waiting open for us, a door which we can walk through easily, but while we are so busy banging on the locked door we don't even notice the open one. My open door was the opportunity to enjoy all the delight of my first child, Sara, without the extra work and distraction of another child; and then, eventually, Michael did arrive, in God's good time. In my book for children called GREAT TEACHERS, I quoted the saying of the Chinese teacher Lao-Tzu, 'When everyone goes along with the Tao, the world is at peace and everyone is happy.' The Tao is the way of the universe, the natural flow of things, God's law at work in all life. However, it is said that it is impossible truly to define what the Tao is, because words immediately bring limitation and the Tao is without limitation, it just *is*.

We can be even happier if we allow the law of Wu Wei to operate in our lives too. Wu Wei literally means 'without doing, causing or making', and in effect this means to allow the natural laws of nature to operate without interference from man. Another interpretation of its meaning is effortless effort, or effort that comes about easily without undue force. So Wu Wei means not trying to force a square peg into a round hole because that is where we feel it ought to fit. We need to accept, without wondering why, that our square peg does not fit there, and quietly await the appearance of the square space instead. The thing we want *will* come, in its own way, in God's time!

This is quite a difficult lesson for me, because I like making plans and, if I have made up my mind to do a particular thing at a certain time, I don't find it easy suddenly to change. I am working on this, however, and gradually learning to be more spontaneous in what I do, so that I can make the best use of things the way they are naturally moving. I am learning that things are much more easily and simply accomplished when done at the right moment.

LEARNING THROUGH NATURE

Inability to go with the natural flow of things, or trying to force our square peg in the round hole, creates a resistance; and resistance creates stress and pain. Taking time to observe nature helps us understand better the principle of flowing and the way in which this brings peace, beauty and harmony to life. There is divine order in nature, and there is also divine order in human life. Inharmony arises because we interfere and resist.

Think of the life-cycle of deciduous trees and the way in which the new, young, green leaves appear, grow to maturity, change colour and then fall and become enriching leaf mould for the soil. This beautiful rhythm flows on, year after year, in perfect harmony. Think of flowers, unfolding gradually and gently from bud to full flower. To resist this natural pattern only destroys it. In Hermann Hesse's classic, SIDDHARTHA, one reads about simple wisdom, expressed beautifully in the description of an old ferryman. His is a wisdom gained through becoming one in spirit with the river and observation of all its ways. We read that he

> was a holy man who for many years believed only in the river and nothing else. He noticed that the river's voice spoke to him. He learned from it; it educated and taught him. The river seemed like a god to him and for many years he did not know that every wind, every cloud, every bird, every beetle is equally divine and knows and can teach just as well as the esteemed river. But when this holy man went off into the woods, he knew everything; he knew more than you and I, without teachers, without books, just because he believed in the river.

LEARNING SERENITY THROUGH PAIN AND ACCEPTANCE

I have a letter in front of me from a friend who has suffered the intense agony of losing a much-loved baby in a cot death. She tells how this heart-breaking tragedy has in fact brought some beautiful gifts into her life:

One thing I learned was compassion. I used not to believe that it was necessary to suffer in order to feel compassion, but now I'm not so sure. I know that I react very differently now when I read or hear about tragedies in the news or to people I know. I feel it with them in a way I didn't before. And so I also realize how we are indeed all one, and that there is unity in all things—my pain is your pain, your joy is my joy.

I learned to live with pain because it was such an intense experience there was nothing I could do, nowhere I could go, where I didn't feel it. So I think I learned something about acceptance because I understood that it was at the interface of my resistance to my baby's death that it hurt the most. I learned on an experiential level that nothing is in itself good or bad, but can be many things at once. I learned gratitude for what I do have, and fully to appreciate the bliss in a 'normal' day, free from disaster and misfortune.

This writing is so touching and direct; it speaks to our hearts of real experience of pain and I believe that there is a gift in these words for us all. The writer's comment, that when she resisted it the pain was worst, is very significant; it is indeed our *resistance* to what is happening which causes so much unhappiness, pain and lack of peace in our lives. It was my resistance to not conceiving when I wanted to which caused me the pain. If I could have said to God, 'Thy will be done', I should not have been in pain. But looking back, I would not have it otherwise, because I learned so many lessons through experiencing the pain of resistance. That pain has helped me become more serene over other issues now. My friend's trauma was far worse than mine, but through this she has learned the wonderful peace of acceptance and discovered, as she so movingly described it, 'the bliss in a normal day free from disaster and misfortune'.

There can be great pain too, of course, in witnessing other people suffer, particularly when they are close to us, and a part of us will always want to rush in and try to take their pain away. If there is nothing we can do, it is helpful to realize that God does know best, and that there is a reason for suffering and pain. If we were able to wave a magic wand and make everything better we might well be denying the other person the very soul lessons which, in their higher self, they most wanted to learn. For the same reason, White Eagle tells us, our spirit teachers and helpers do not interfere with our karma and our opportunity to grow through it. Instead they give us their constant, loving support. But this support is given dispassionately, without any distress attached to it. As White Eagle says (in his book PRAYER IN THE NEW AGE), 'The Master helps you by helping you command yourself.' So, when you are faced with the ordeal of supporting a dear one in his or her pain, go to the God within and ask that you may be filled with serenity and confidence in the beautiful plan which is working out in your loved one's life, so that you can give your true and loving support, unclouded by any emotional distress.

FLOWING BRINGS CHANGE AND CHANGE BRINGS GROWTH

If we can learn to accept God's will serenely and learn to go with the natural flow of things, gradually we let go of our resistance and can accept that life is always changing. Nature never stands still; the flower, the tree, the river is ever changing. If they did not change, much of their beauty and magic would be lost. Yet in human life we often find change extremely painful and hard to cope with, and we resist it desperately—especially anything which seems to threaten our fundamental security.

The change which the death of a close loved one brings is often very hard to cope with, even if we believe totally in life continuing after death, for the physical loss is always felt keenly in our little self, and we need to allow ourselves the space to mourn that loss and be comforted at a very human level. I certainly found this after my father died.

Tears are healing and not a sign of weakness. To cry is a way of encouraging the healing of the hurt little self, so my advice is not to resist your tears, but to give your little self loving support as it grieves. All loss has a beautiful gift within it, hidden by the pain, to be found when we are ready. In another part of my friend's writing about the pain of her baby's loss, she explains how it has taught her about what she calls 'the miracle of death'.

I came to appreciate the reality of death and also to have some insights about death. Somehow my baby's death made me realize with absolute certainty that there is no death, that death is perfect—it is perfect to be born and wholly appropriate to die, that death is also a miracle (as well as birth) and a new beginning. His death put me in touch with the spirit life in a very direct way for me, as if he opened up a door for me that cannot be closed by passing into the world of light from this one. Since he's died, I've felt a certainty in the spirit that I didn't have before.

ANOTHER ASPECT OF PEACE

Being willing to accept change in our lives and move spontaneously with the energy of the moment helps us find inner peace;

but we also need to consider the dynamic aspect of peace. This is highlighted by some words of White Eagle's in GOLDEN HARVEST, 'Peace is a dynamic power. From the heart of peace comes right action.' But notice that he says 'from the heart of peace'. It is from that peaceful centre, which is achieved through being able to flow with things as they are, that eventually wise action can come.

In order to be wise and loving, guided by the true Christ-self, rather than the anxious, impatient little self, action usually needs to flow out of the feminine, gentle, yielding centre of peace. An inner contact with ourselves, beside our own 'lake of peace' in meditation, helps us become more clearly aware of the wisdom which will guide our future actions. White Eagle tells us:

> Man has to seek first the kingdom of heaven, the place of stillness and quiet at the highest level of which he is capable, and then the heavenly influences can pour into him, recreate him and use him for the salvation of mankind. (p. 49)

After our inner communion by the lake of peace, the time usually comes when we need to embrace our masculine energy and take positive, dynamic action, clearly directed by the Christ within. If all our action stems from this centre of peace, it will be incisive, powerful and perfectly timed. I believe that being peaceful does not always mean being still and controlled, but it does mean aspiring to act always from a still centre. There are times when we want to dance and sing and laugh—to feel joy and be uninhibited. If we are connected with our inner centre of peace, then when we wish to 'let our hair down' our energy will flow from the creative, dynamic, joyful and exuberant spirit within. From deep peace comes creative expression, for at the inner centre of our being all positive feelings meet: divine power, wisdom, love, joy and peace are one.

72

WAYS TO FIND PEACE

Here are some points I have found useful to remember in my endeavours to be peaceful no matter what is going on around me:

1. Trust in God

I believe that lack of inner peace implies a lack of trust in God and His great plan for our lives and the life of all humanity (see the quotation from the teacher Emmanuel in the final chapter!). The more totally we can trust in God, the more we are at peace.

Every time you find yourself in a turmoil, fearful or battered by outer conditions, affirm:

I am at peace, I trust in God.

2. Surrender to God

Lack of inner peace can stem from holding on too tightly to our own idea of

—how we would like things to be

—when we would like something to happen

—when we feel it 'should' happen

—what someone else 'should' be doing.

But if we can just let go of the matter and leave it to God, there is an enormous feeling of relief, release—and peace.

3. Willingness to change

Affirm in your heart your willingness to let all preconceived ideas go, and your readiness to step forward into new joy. *I am willing to change.*

4. 'Let nothing disturb you'—be the master of yourself

White Eagle tells us (p. 46) that 'A Master is never perturbed' and he helps us realize that we can be like this, too: we can be master in the lodge of our own inner being (p. 40).*

5. *I affirm peace*
I have found that affirmations are one of the most powerful tools available to help us see clearly through the turmoil of the little self and become at peace, master of our own lodge. They can be used often, at any time of the day or night, and

—said out loud or in the heart

—written down

—put up in places where they will continually catch the attention.

The affirmations given on page 77 are ones which I think can be specially helpful in discovering inner peace.

*White Eagle often uses the word 'lodge' (which means a communal tent or wigwam as well as a sanctuary or meeting place) in this way, rather as he might say 'ruler of your own inner kingdom'.

THE SIX-POINTED STAR (4)

Every day on awaking and many times during the day, particularly when you are being overwhelmed and harassed by the affairs of the physical life, pause and remember that it is the little self, the human personality, which is being tried, and then understand that above you in the invisible realms is that greater self, the Christ-self. Look into that form of glorious colour, that radiant life, and you will feel infinite power flowing into your personality. You will be conscious, above your personality, of a self which is limitless, which is living in God. (p. 47)

 The little self feels disturbed and fearful so it is not at peace, but (p. 45) 'by an effort of the Will of God within', it becomes aware of the greater 'Christ-self'.

 The Christ-self can then heal and uplift the troubled little self. 'Come, brother, come above the mists, come unto me, and I will give you that inner peace for which you long.' (p. 41)

 'Whatever ordeal lies before you, remember the Christ presence: *Lo! I am with you always.'* (p. 38)

Try to remember: *A master is never perturbed.*

A MEDITATION ON 'THE MASTER
SOUL IS CALM, QUIET AND STEADY'

Daily seek for that still centre within your soul which is the abiding place of the Christ-spirit. (p. 45)

Come in thought into your quiet, inner sanctuary. Kneel before the simple white altar and gaze at the little light which burns there quietly, steadily, eternally.

Affirm: *I am calm, quiet and steady.... I am master of my lodge.... I am divine peace.*

If necessary, keep on and on repeating these words. They will help to calm down your emotions and still your mind so that you can open your heart and your whole being to the heavenly peace which will come flooding into you.

As you start to feel more peaceful, open your awareness to your teacher's presence. He/she is with you in your inner sanctuary. His/her serenity helps you reconnect more strongly with your own serenity.... When you are ready, take your teacher's hand and go together into the inner garden, to sit by the lotus pool. The water is still and clear and reflects the blue sky and sunlight....

There is a fragrance in the air, which helps you relax even more as together you watch the pure white lotus which floats on the water. Watch it gradually unfold its petals in the sunlight to reveal its golden centre.... Here, deep in the still centre, when all is at peace, the flame of heavenly truth is revealed.

Meditate on this picture and feel that flame of truth and peace stir in your soul ... feel it grow strong and bright and fill you with both security and strength. Use whichever of the affirmations for inner peace feels most appropriate for you while you are here in this quiet sanctuary.

AFFIRMATIONS (4)

As usual, here are some suggestions for affirmations on the theme of this chapter. Remember that you can also make up your own. Try above all to speak with your deepest self through the use of the affirmation, and not to make the affirmation too limiting in its application.

I affirm peace
I am calm, quiet and steady
I am divine peace
I am at peace. I trust in God
I am master of my lodge. Nothing disturbs me. What I cannot do, I hand back to God
God knows my need
I flow with things as they are
'I live today with God, and my future is filled with joy'
'Peace is a dynamic power. From the heart of peace comes right action.

5

THE MASTER SOUL
IS STRONG TO SERVE

You know not the day nor the hour when the Master will come.

I LOVE THESE words; they always touch my heart in a magical way. Life is full of magic and miracles! Life is full of glorious opportunities for happiness and joyful service, if we are open to what is before us. There is an old English legend which clearly illustrates the spiritual truth that our opportunity to serve often comes in disguise and not in the form we might expect. It tells the origin of a beautiful lake in the dales of northern Yorkshire, a lake I know well.

Once upon a time an elderly couple were living in a little house on the outskirts of a village. They lived a life of great devotion to each other. On a stormy night they heard a knock at their door and found an old man standing there, huddled in a cloak, trying to protect himself from the violent downpour and terrible wind. 'Please let me come in and shelter for the night', he said, 'I have knocked at every door and no-one would invite me in.'

'Of course you must come in and shelter', said the couple, and they took him indoors to dry himself by their fire. They invited him to share their simple supper, and rest on their couch. The next morning when they looked into the stranger's eyes, they saw the greatest love and light they had ever known. 'Who is this we have sheltered?', they wondered.

In return for their hospitality the stranger said he had the power to grant their dearest wish. They asked to be allowed to die together and never be separated. 'I can grant you this', said the stranger, 'for I can take you both with me now, into a new world of light.' Taking their hands he led them into the sunlight of a new day; and when the old couple looked back they saw all their village had been covered during the night by the waters of a great flood, but the water had stopped just at their doorway.

There are many other stories, legends and fairy tales which tell of good fairies and saints disguising themselves, and only revealing their true beauty and identity when they have tested the hero or heroine's worth and goodness (this very one is similar to a classical story in which the couple are turned into trees whose branches intertwine, while the rest of the community is flooded). I think there is a lesson for us all in this legend. Things are not always as they seem, and our opportunities to give love and service may occur in strange and unexpected ways. Indeed, service is not always what we think it might be.

WHAT IS SERVICE?

In this section of THE QUIET MIND White Eagle tells us that service is:

—'to dwell continually upon the love of God' (p. 53)

—to 'train yourself to recognize God's goodness working through everyone else' (p. 54)

—'to hold fast to the good, the true and the beautiful' (p. 52)

—'continually to think aright—continually to send forth love, to forgive' (p. 57)

—remembering that 'whatever your occupation ... it is a form of service' (p. 57)

—working 'hand-in-hand with God' (p. 57)

—being 'thankful for every opportunity to serve which is laid before you'. (p. 57)

The first four of these sayings highlight the most important aspect of service which, paradoxically, is the one we are most likely to forget. Our western culture is so orientated towards doing, that we tend to forget the power of being, a fact known so well by the yogis of the East. There is a story about Gautama Buddha which I particularly like. One day many of his followers had gathered on Vulture Peak expecting him to teach them. Instead he sat before them for a long time in total silence. When eventually he raised a flower in his hand, still without saying a word, everyone was amazed, but one disciple smiled with joy because through the simplicity of Buddha's action and non-action he received his 'great awakening'.

Most people equate helping others and serving with actually doing things. But here White Eagle tells us that we are being of service by dwelling 'continually upon the love of God'.

How can we do this? If we remember that our primary purpose in meditation is to grow more and more aware of God and allow the divine love to shine ever more clearly through all we say and do and are, it becomes clear that the regular practice of meditation is a way in which we can train and encourage ourselves to dwell often on the love of God. The more that meditation becomes a part of our life's routine (even if we are not aware of anything remarkable happening as we sit) the more we are putting ourselves in touch with God's love. In White Eagle's way of meditation we are taught to concentrate upon a symbol of beauty and devotion, such as a rose, a lotus, a still pool, or the star. This very concentration works in a subtle way to train our thoughts and our whole consciousness. It encourages us, as White Eagle says, 'to hold fast to the good, the true and the beautiful'.

Thankfulness is also a form of service akin more to being than doing. It opens the gate to joy and helps put us back into touch with God's love and light in our hearts. In the fourth saying I quoted, White Eagle tells us that continually sending forth love and forgiveness is a form of service too. We can thus take thankfulness a stage further, when we send the thought into the world in a deliberate way, as we do in the work of the projection of the light within that White Eagle has taught us. In this healing, the star symbol is used as a focal point to channel light or love to those in need and to the whole world. We are taught to visualize a blazing six-pointed star filled with light and radiating God's healing power to all humanity and to all creation.* There is special power attached to the star symbol itself, for it is an ancient symbol (given us originally at the direction of the illumined brethren for whom White Eagle is a spokesman, in the way described in the Preface). It works in a magical way to lift our consciousness above the earth and inspire the awakening of the seed of Christ-consciousness, the light of God, within our hearts. It is this awakening of the Christ within all mankind which is prompting the movement towards brotherhood in our world today.

This form of service involves working in partnership with God, 'hand-in-hand with God'. All our service becomes a partnership with God, the more we allow His light and love to

*A free leaflet which describes this work, entitled 'There is something you can do—now!', is available from The White Eagle Publishing Trust.

shine clearly through us without obstacle or obstruction. (This we do by bringing our higher selves through into everyday consciousness, in the ways described throughout this book.) All creation is a part of God and all creation is thus linked by God's love and light. It therefore follows that every effort we make to serve any part of God's creation, or to unite ourselves more completely with God's love, is in fact service to all life.

Nowadays, as I remarked before, the way in which all nature is interdependent at a physical level and how, through human ignorance its delicate balance can be upset, is becoming much more widely recognized. At an inner level, too, all life is linked, and the more we can be aware of this unity, the more we realize the value of every effort we individually make. White Eagle says,

> You cannot make one effort towards heaven without the whole of the world, even the very earth itself, being the better for it. See the responsibility that lies with you, brethren! What a glorious opportunity is yours! Don't allow the darkness of earth to deny you your birthright of freedom and happiness, of service and worship. (p. 53)

The interconnectedness of all life is an inspiring thought, especially in the context of service. White Eagle teaches us that we all reincarnate in groups, linked together by karmic bonds, and thus have special opportunities to serve and help each other. As we grow, so in a wonderful way we help everyone else to grow. This is especially true of those with whom we have close karmic links, but it also applies to the whole brotherhood of life. As well as in our inner spiritual bonding, we are linked by the elements, by the very substance of our physical bodies and the influences active within us which make up our personalities. We are also linked to all nature and the angelic kingdom. White Eagle's teaching helps us open our awareness to our angelic brethren and reminds of our opportunity to work in partnership and brother-hood with them. I feel that one of the reasons he chose a native American personality for his work of teaching in this day of life is that it brought with it a particular vibration which is totally in harmony with nature and the angelic kingdom, and thus also stirs our sleeping knowledge of brotherhood with nature.

There is much still to be reawakened in our hearts about our kinship with life; it is something which we gradually discover in ourselves. The discovery cannot be forced: it is not a question of acquiring specific mental knowledge, which is of the brain, for this is an issue of the heart. It comes about slowly, as the aspirant follows the path and develops the intuition, and the soul's love and wisdom unfold. White Eagle helps us in this process by giving us the opportunity to serve in his Absent Healing work, using words both beautiful and mantramistic (that is, the words have power through their very repetition), which enable us to work in partnership with the angels. No special qualities are required in order to serve in this way, except a simple, loving heart, a willingness to keep to our path, and, of course, a true desire to serve and 'keep on keeping on'. Often it is a question of doing this faithfully without spectacular results, for spiritual service is slow but sure.*

PRINCIPLES OF SERVICE

Service ... is often humdrum
White Eagle reminds us that our service lies in every condition in our lives now, rather than in some distant future when the grand call to service will suddenly come. The teacher Emmanuel

*If you would like more details of this work, write for the leaflet 'Joining in the White Eagle healing work'

does the same when he says that 'sitting with the circumstances of our lives' is in itself getting on with our lives.* Sometimes our service is unexciting and unromantic, but White Eagle tells us:

> However humble or even humdrum your work may be to you, it is *your* special appointment, and through your work on earth you can make your contribution to the happiness of all. (p. 57)

This lesson was brought home to me when I got into conversation with a painter who was repainting all the seats at one of my favourite seaside places. His job was simple, some might say humdrum, and yet he was putting his whole heart into his work and taking great pride in making the seats look good. The light shone radiantly from his heart as he spoke to me, and I am sure it permeated his work so that in a subtle way it would uplift all those who sat there in the weeks ahead. I love Brother Lawrence's well-known words from the seventeenth century:

> The time of business ... does not with me differ from the time of prayer; and in the noise and clutter of my kitchen, while several persons are at the same time calling for different things, I possess God in as great tranquillity as if I were upon my knees at the Blessed Sacrament.

One of the purposes of our lives on earth is to bring the light into every condition of earthly life, and thus to transmute the heaviness of earth into light and aliveness, into creativity and joy.

Service ... is joyful
Sometimes we can allow our service to become heavy and burdensome, and we keep going simply because it seems to be our duty and what we 'should' be doing, when all the spontaneity and delight seem to have evaporated away. If this happens, the

*For a note on Emmanuel see page 142

84

first thing to do is ask, 'Is this service really being asked of me?', because there *are* times when what we think of as service is purely habit. On such occasions it may be more important to remember to serve the God within than to punish the self with devotion to some outward thing which has ceased to need the attention we have been giving it. There is more of God in spontaneity than in habit! However, if we look into our hearts and find that the service we are offering is important to us, but that we are simply having a problem connecting to the original purpose, then it can be helpful to think of it first as service to God, and see where that thought leads us. To see it in this way is a means of bringing ourselves back into touch with the spontaneous joy of His light and love, both within our own heart and within the heart of all creation.

If your service seems a burden, it may be a sign that the character of the service needs to change. However, if it is not so much that it is burdensome as that it is difficult to go through with a chosen course, try concentrating all your attention on this one day only. Don't think of what may have felt like endless days ahead. Instead, look for the fun and playful moments you can find in each experience. This is just a thought. You will be amazed at how much happiness there is hidden away in the most unexpected places. Remember also to be open to change. There is a moment when the character of your life *will* alter—a new job, a change of neighbourhood—and it is in the *inner* openness to the divine will, not in being tied to a form of doing, that the real service lies.

I experienced the need for change when I realized I had to ask for a sabbatical. The days had begun to stretch ahead in a ceaseless round of duty. But the realization came that I could serve in a different way, through the recreative benefits of being away from the work for a period. I asked for the co-operation of my family and colleagues, and succeeded in finding the release I sought. When I came back after a year of travel, everything was fulfilling for me once more, and I knew I was bringing back a special gift to my work, through my renewed happiness in my service, and the understanding I had gained of other cultures, religions and ways of being.

Service ... is sometimes hanging on by the skin of your teeth when the challenges are coming thick and fast!

Try never to sit in judgment on yourself over the effectiveness of your attempts to serve. Our opportunities for service can come in many different packages. Our maximum ability to respond to each may seem feeble in our own estimation, in comparison with what we feel that everyone else is doing. But I find it helpful to remember that we are each unique, in a unique situation, with unique challenges, and what is right for us and the best we can do in a particular circumstance may be quite different from what is right for someone else and what they appear to be doing. So: don't compare and don't judge. Just do your best. Love yourself, even when you think you have failed to do your best, but never give up.

Sometimes conditions are so challenging—both outwardly and inwardly—that all we can do, metaphorically speaking, is to hang on by the skin of our teeth and just keep remembering our link with the star, or with our master, or our inner contact in whatever form it comes. We all go through dark nights of the soul when it seems impossible to maintain any form of spiritual insight into our own lives, let alone any awareness of the light shining forth to help others. But White Eagle says always to 'keep on keeping on' at these times—even if the spiritual contact we are trying to make seems like just a few minutes of heavy-hearted effort in which nothing happens. If we do hang on, one day the magic will work and we will truly feel the light fill our heart once more. Meanwhile, our very struggle to keep the light burning during a time of crucifixion is perhaps doing as much if not more than when we are hitting the high spots and feeling we really are getting somewhere.

A friend wrote to me about her struggles and has agreed that I may quote a part of her letter:

> I am finding life desperately difficult just now. My husband lost his job and although he has a new one, that is very uncertain too, and everything has been getting steadily more difficult. It has taken huge efforts on my part to keep everything running smoothly and to ensure the children's lives remain unaffected. It has also meant I have had to return to work full time. I have become so weary with all the struggle and my faith is at a very low ebb. I am finding it increasingly difficult to do any meditation at all, and usually I feel totally turned off. Sheer exhaustion has made me lose interest and it grieves me that I feel neither able to give nor to feel.

I have shared this in the hope that if you identify with her difficulties, you will be easy with your own little self and also not give up your efforts to hang on to whatever form your spiritual endeavour takes. One day you will find your world has changed, and you will truly see the result of keeping on keeping on through the darkest storms. What I suggested to my friend was to try and keep a short contact with her Source, but not to push and struggle to do anything more until her outer life was less stressful. It seemed far better that she should allow a little space for relaxation for herself and feel reassured that working for harmony and happiness in her family *is* her spiritual service at the moment. I also suggested that her meditation time might take the form of a relaxation and visualization which was totally enjoyable for her, and in no way a struggle: for example, relaxation in bed, listening to her favourite music—or visualizing that she was a bird flying free in the sunlight, right up into the heart of the light, and then flying out all over the world, taking the light and letting it shine forth wherever she flew.

Service ... can be simple and spontaneous

Service does not have to be some big and complicated task which goes on for a long time. Simple, spur-of-the-moment acts can give service which might have far-reaching effects. Have you ever experienced how a warm and happy greeting or smile from a stranger on a day when you were feeling sad can uplift you? Something like this can make an enormous difference to how you feel. I like the saying, 'If you see someone without a smile, give them one of yours.' Smiles and kindnesses are catching and are very simple ways we can pass on a little ray of happiness. Spontaneous gestures of thoughtfulness to one another, however small, can ease all sorts of difficulties in relationships. Often it only takes a small step of conciliation to mend a strained friendship. Little acts of kindness, which individually may seem trivial, can accumulate until they form a notable contribution to the overall light and joy in the world.

Service ... can mean do it now—not tomorrow!

Many of us have a natural human response to prevaricate and decide to leave something we feel urged to do 'until tomorrow' or 'when I feel more like it'. But perhaps 'tomorrow' will never come, or when it does, it will be too late to take up the opportunity that had been offered? Sometimes we leave things because we are too weary, or just too lazy; sometimes because we are not confident enough that our intuition to do something is correct.

I was taught the lesson of 'doing it now' and learning to trust and act on my intuition in a rather sad way. Some years ago, on a cold winter's day, I spontaneously decided to treat myself to a bunch of fragrant spring flowers. When I was at home arranging them, my inner voice said, 'Buy some for Madge too.' Madge was my mother-in-law, and I was visiting her that day, for we always went to tea with her on Fridays, after I had collected the children from school. On this particular Friday the weather was very poor and I could not face going off in another direction after school and having to struggle with parking. I did not completely ignore the inner voice, and I said to myself, 'I'll buy Madge the flowers next week.' But by the next Friday I had lost my chance, for Madge had died. She passed on very suddenly and unexpectedly. Her passing was wonderful for her, and a joyous reunion with her beloved husband in spirit, but this episode taught me something which I shall never forget.

However, I also learned that though it is good to do something right now, if possible, nonetheless if we don't—for whatever reason—we need not 'beat ourselves up' for it, because our so-called failure can turn out to be an opportunity to learn something else. In this case I had a beautiful contact with Madge when I gave her a bunch of flowers in spirit, and without doubt my aching heart (aching because I had not given them earlier and in time) deepened the inner communion I experienced with her in the spirit state of life.

A friend recently told me a similar story of how she was very distressed because she felt she had let her brother down, when at the time of their mother's passing she had been unable to answer his question, 'Why does it have to be like this?' Although she trusted utterly in God's perfect plan and timing, she was unable to find any words at that moment. Later she prayed that White Eagle would help her give her brother the proof and comfort for which he longed. After a period of time this did come about, in a remarkable way which was much more evidential. It happened like this. My mother had suddenly been inspired to write to her with a message from my father in spirit, saying that he had met her mother and how radiant and happy she was. My mother knew nothing (in her conscious self) of my friend's prayer. The message, because of the way in which it came, was more meaningful to her brother than any statement of belief from her own lips could have been.

Service ... is sometimes of an unexpected kind
Quite often the nature of our service does not turn out to be at all what we were expecting. Sometimes we are so set in our thoughts and hopes of having the chance to serve life in a particular way that we do not see the opportunity which is already waiting before us. White Eagle encourages us:

> It does not matter what your work is on the earth. What does matter is that you should do your work with all your heart and with all your strength and with all your mind. (p. 52)

Some years ago, as we were working on an *asana* in a yoga class, the teacher said he wanted us to do it as though it were the very last thing we would be doing in this lifetime, and how we would always be remembered. I suddenly realized how often I did something in a half-hearted way, without putting one hundred per cent effort into it, perhaps with the thought at the back of my mind that on another occasion I should feel more in the mood and do it better. This teacher's remark certainly pulled me up and encouraged me to stay in the present moment more, instead of doing things without full attention while I dreamt of more exciting moments in the future!

Service ... can mean just 'keeping on keeping on'

It is a good idea not to be in too much of a hurry about spiritual matters. It is easy to get carried away and want everything to happen quickly—to want, metaphorically speaking, to storm the gates of heaven. But as White Eagle gently reminds us, 'Flowers do not force their way with great strife. Flowers open to perfection slowly in the sun.' (p. 58)

Spiritual service time and again means quietly keeping on keeping on without many visible results. A very good example of this is when we are sending healing thoughts to another person. The human tendency is to look for results and progress, but progress in spiritual matters is usually well hidden from the little self's perception. This is all part of God's wise plan for our growth, because it stops the little self from becoming inflated with what it can delude itself are its own abilities. The path of karma yoga, as defined in the East, means doing service for its own sake, without thought of the possible results. If our service is truly motivated by the God in our heart we will not worry about results as long as we know we have done the very best we can.

Service ... can mean sacrifice—but all sacrifice brings ultimate joy (the rose blooms on the cross)

The rose blooming on the cross is an age-old mystical symbol for the beautiful opening of the heart centre which so often, in the great scheme of things, comes after sacrifice and pain. Out of the suffering comes the indescribable blessing of a deeper understanding and enfolding love, which is the essence of true

91

happiness. In a small way, I experienced this in the episode of Madge and the flowers. The vow of the Boddhisattva, often quoted, is a conscious wish to allow the rose of love to bloom on the cross of sacrifice. The Boddhisattva gives up any desire for personal liberation in the devotion of his/her entire life to helping others. The vow is to sacrifice personal liberation until all sentient beings are free from suffering.

Often service demands a certain letting go of self, and this can be a very subtle demand. It might be letting go of spiritual pride, of our desire to serve in a way which we think is very spiritual. For example—serving as a healer might be our goal, and we may throw ourselves into it, and then find that we are offering our help without anyone taking it up. However, our real patients may be the sad and overstressed colleagues we are among, or the little children with whom we struggle to be patient, or the friends whose anger we help to soften by our example. Sometimes it is only once we sacrifice, or let go, our blinkered idea of what we call service, that we can realize the true beauty and fulfilment of the opportunities which lie before us.

These opportunities, which may outwardly seem limited and boring, may in fact be the very openings our true self has chosen for our spiritual growth in this lifetime. For example, we may find ourselves in very restricted and lonely circumstances, when the one thing we really want to do is be out there in the world among lots of people with many opportunities to be of visible human service. But in fact, the lesson we may need to learn is that through physical loneliness we can come to realize our true relationship and oneness with God and the power and reality of service on the inner planes.

Any act of letting go brings its own gift, and a letting go of a set idea about service, or what is worthwhile for us to be doing, is no exception. So if you release a treasured idea about how things should be for you and instead embrace one hundred per cent the opportunity of the moment, there is always a return in full measure. The divine law of compensation works unfailingly, White Eagle says. 'When love possesses your heart, all service, all giving, brings such joy that there is no sacrifice' (p. 56).

THE SIX-POINTED STAR (5)

If you endeavour to raise the Christ within you, you help to raise all mankind. You cannot make one effort towards heaven without the whole of the world, even the very earth itself, being the better for it. (p. 53)

 Service is practical. It starts at home—in every condition and relationship, in every thought and action.

 The more we keep attuned to the inner guiding light, the more the great light can fill our whole being, and every aspect of our lives.

 So we shine like the star and radiate the Christ healing power, its love and light, through everything we say and do and are.

A MEDITATION ON 'THE MASTER SOUL IS STRONG TO SERVE'

Keep the Light burning. There is nothing more important than to keep the Christ Light burning within. Only this will give you the power that you need to do those little acts of service that the Master asks of you. (p. 51)

Picture the symbol of the six-pointed star (or if you find this a problem, picture the Sun and have the thought of the star in your mind) and breathe in its radiant light. Offer yourself, in service, to God. Let go of all preconceived thoughts about what form that service might take. Just rest quietly in the inner centre of your being, and feel the light, still and radiant, a bright flame in your heart. In a magical way it is linked to the great star above, and as you breathe in the light, your flame grows bigger and bigger until it becomes a pyramid of light which reaches up to touch the star above. When this happens, you too are lifted up, so that you become absorbed in the light of the star and enter a carefree world of light and joy.

Allow your visualization to unfold in whatever way is most helpful to you. Maybe your spirit teacher will show you a particular act of service you can do for someone on earth, or maybe you will gain clearer insight about the work you are already doing. Do not try to force this in any way. If nothing comes to you, know that through your inner attunement to the Christ-principle, the star, you are serving God in *whatever* you do. Pray that you will always follow the light that lights your way.

When the time comes to 'breathe your way back to earth', very deliberately breathe back with you the strength, peace and inspiration of the star, so that you are ready to tackle the tasks that lie in front of you with renewed energy and joy.

AFFIRMATIONS (5)

I am strong to serve
I follow my inner light
I am ready at all times to serve my inner master
I have all the strength and courage I need for anything God asks of me
I send forth love and forgiveness
I can serve God in simple ways
Every job I do can be my service to God
I work hand-in-hand with God
I hold fast to the good, the true and the beautiful.

6

THE MASTER SOUL IS
WISE IN SPEECH AND ACTION

Through an ever-increasing love in the heart you will grow wise.

IT IS EASY to assume that someone who has intellectual knowledge is also wise, but that is not always so. A person who has had much intellectual opportunity and experience can lack heart-understanding, and someone who has no mental training can be truly wise. In chapter four, I quoted a passage about a wise ferryman from Hermann Hesse's novel SIDDHARTHA. This ferryman had no intellectual knowledge and yet was the wisest person Siddhartha had met: 'He knew everything ... without teachers, without books, just because he believed in the river.' And when Siddhartha was opening his troubled heart to him, he found the ferryman the most wonderful and attentive listener he had ever known:

He mentioned everything, he could tell him everything, even the most painful things....

As he went on speaking and Vasudeva listened to him with a serene face, Siddhartha was more keenly aware than ever of Vasudeva's attentiveness. He felt his troubles, his anxieties and his secret hopes flow across to him and then return again.

Disclosing his wound to his listener was the same as bathing it in the river, until it became cool and one with the river. As he went on talking and confessing, Siddhartha felt more and more that this was no longer Vasudeva, no longer a man who was listening to him. He felt that this motionless listener was absorbing his confession as a tree absorbs the rain, that this motionless man was the river itself, that he was God Himself, that he was eternity itself.

WISDOM IS BEING ABLE TO LISTEN

A wise old owl sat in an oak.
The more he saw, the less he spoke.
The less he spoke, the more he heard:
Why can't we be like that wise old bird?
Traditional English Rhyme

Can you imagine being like Siddhartha's old ferryman? Being able to listen with total attentiveness, without any of your own beliefs and ideas about how things ought to be getting in the way? A master would listen to you like this, just as the old ferryman listened to Siddhartha. We all have the capacity to listen to our brother or our sister in this way. In another book, THE GENTLE BROTHER, White Eagle gives us some advice about listening:

How often do you listen to a conversation and absorb nothing? The conversation may seem to you to be futile— but perhaps *you* are the foolish one. Forget everything else but your companion as you are conversing with him. Concentrate your whole attention on what he is saying. Courtesy at least demands this. If the Master should come, and you, not knowing it was he, talked to him—possibly foolishly—the Master would take notice of your every word. For the time being your conversation would be all that mattered to him. Take this very seriously, because it offers a practical and simple method of thought control. Centre your whole attention on what you are doing, always.

I used to think I listened, but more recently I have come to realize how little I did really listen. Having an impatient personality, I was so busy with the next thing on my mind, I did not give the actual moment my full attention. At other times, I realized, my attention was so full up with my own feeling and opinions about the matter that I did not actually 'hear' what the other person was saying. Real listening requires a lot of effort—it doesn't just happen. We need to train ourselves to listen, just as we have to train ourselves to do many other worthwhile things. It is a process of 'keeping on keeping on' watching and noting, 'I was not really listening then; my attention wandered off'; and then bringing oneself back to this moment of *now*. As White Eagle says, it can be a practical exercise in thought-control, and wonderful training for meditation.

The more we can train ourselves to listen to our brother, the more easily we shall be able to listen to God, to our inner guidance. We are more likely to be able to 'hear' the inner voice if we have been able to empty the cup of our everyday consciousness: to empty it at least of set ideas, opinions, judgments, fears, and so on. They are blocks which get in the way of our true listening, hearing and loving. Again, loving is the key; the more we are able to work from the loving place in our hearts, the more we are working from our true self, and so the more we are truly interested in what our brother, our sister is saying.

We need to be wise in how we speak, of course, as well as how we listen. Sharp or thoughtless words or idle criticism and gossip cause unnecessary pain. In our true selves we have the strength and wisdom to avoid getting into critical discussions about others, and gossip. The way to contact the true self when such strength is needed is to ask inwardly for help. You may be surprised at the way the help comes and how easy it becomes to steer things into more constructive channels. Sometimes the answer is to have the courage to say quietly and clearly, but not critically, something like, 'I don't feel comfortable about discussing Mary in her absence; I'm sure we don't understand the whole story from her point of view. Can we talk about something else?'

I have found it helpful to memorize the words which were given to the original Polaire brethren (the forerunners of our present-day White Eagle Star Brotherhood):

>Speak to your brother of the aims you have in common;
>Sympathize with his suffering, share his joys:
>But be blind, deaf and dumb to all outside this triangle of true brotherhood.

WISDOM IS BEING GENTLE, LOVING AND KIND

Wisdom is like a jewel, with a still flame at its centre. The flame is God; the jewel of God's wisdom has many facets. Included among those facets are all the qualities of a master which are listed in THE QUIET MIND. But certainly one of the most important qualities which leads us to wisdom is love. True wisdom is always gentle and kind. It leads to an unfolding of the gentle, intuitive wisdom of the heart, rather than the arrogant opinions and judgments of the head mind. This loving wisdom comes from knowing that when we hurt another, we hurt the whole world and eventually ourselves. It comes from knowing that we cannot judge anyone and that all souls are trying to find their way 'home', that is, heavenwards—even though the way there may take them into circumstances which seem odd or break social conventions at times, and perhaps through the vehicle of a personality which does just that. No matter how justified we think we may be in our judgment, we always need to step back in order to allow divine wisdom to unfold, and to be gentle in all we say and do.

WISDOM IS YIELDING

Being wise means being humble enough to know that we may not always, nor even often, 'get it right'; and that we must always be prepared to back down and be still and listen. A master's wisdom is gentle and yielding, not hard and rigid. It is not bounded by the limitations of earthly understanding and it is free and clear. It flows with circumstances like the waters of a great river; it never tries to force its way against the current. Being wise can mean standing back to allow others to come to their own realizations without interference; being wise is always to act in love, and to know that sometimes not to act at all is the most loving thing to do.

Above all, being wise is most definitely *not* dependent on possessing a store of intellectual knowledge. Wisdom is not attained through the intellect. In PRAYER IN THE NEW AGE, White Eagle tells us:

Man tries to understand God with his intellect, and he reads books and others' opinions, he analyses and criticizes and thinks he has arrived at truth.

But that is not the way, my friends; the way to truth is the way of the spirit, is the way of the light from within man's heart. It is to understand and unfold all those spiritual faculties with which God has endowed his son–daughter on this earth plane. It is by way of meditation and contemplation, as the saints taught. But even this is not enough. Man may meditate all his life on the glories of the heaven world and still be unable to reach his goal. God intended man on earth to be perfectly balanced between spirit and matter, between the divine life and the material life. Hence the symbol of the star, representing the perfectly balanced man, and representing too the Christ-spirit which must find expression in daily life, in gentleness, in humility, kindness and courtesy, in accepting God as the one true source of life. Side by side with your communion, it is in your effort to serve and from your human experience that you will gain entry into the mysteries of life.

Sometimes we make the mistake of equating mental study or knowledge of spiritual ideas with spiritual advancement. But, as White Eagle says, 'that is not the way'.

Some of the greatest, wisest and most saintly human beings, as Siddhartha found, are those who have no intellectual knowledge at all, and have an almost childlike simplicity. As Jesus said, *'Whosoever shall not receive the kingdom of God as a little child, shall in no wise enter therein'*. And in the book ZEN FOR BEGINNERS we are told:

Zen practice is for people who don't mind always being at the beginning, because every moment is new, which means that we are new, because we are not separate from the moment.

And again:

Zen masters speak a lot about 'beginner's mind'. In Zen practice we are trying to become beginners, to experience life without the interference of our whole accumulation of opinions and ideas.

The implication is clear: if you can follow spontaneously and entirely the simple wisdom of your heart, throw away this book! You may remember the quotation from THE QUIET MIND that I began with, on page 17. But I hope that what I have written, and the passages I've quoted, *will* nonetheless help you in the direction of your own inner wisdom.

WISDOM IS BEING SIMPLE

White Eagle's teaching is very much in harmony with Zen thought; indeed, as I have said in my Preface, I am sometimes aware of him in the dress of a Zen master. He tells us that it is a natural characteristic of our body-mind to want to grasp lots of intellectual facts, but it often becomes greedy for them and is as prone to indigestion as the body itself is. I think that over a period of many incarnations, in order to develop the mind as a useful tool but at the same time cultivate humility and simplicity, we all return from time to time with highly-developed mental faculties, and at other times with the reverse. Zen masters teach their pupils to get beyond thought and learn about 'the ultimate reality' by experiencing totally the concrete reality of every day, and being one with simple things.

There are many stories of the seemingly simple way in which disciples became enlightened. For example, we are told how the great Japanese poet Basho was intellectually extremely clever and discoursed at length to his master about the *sutras* (the scriptures) he had read. One day his master told him that he wanted to hear one sentence of his own words, 'the words of your true self'. At this Basho was struck dumb. He could not think of anything which was essentially his own. Then suddenly there was a sound in the monastery garden and Basho turned to his master and said:

> Still pond.
> A frog jumps in
> Kerplunk!

His master laughed and told him, 'These are the words of your true self.' Basho laughed too, for in that moment he had attained enlightenment.

Zen students are also taught to empty their minds of busy thought. In another story we hear how the fifth Patriarch of Zen set his disciples a poetry competition. The most learned monk, who was expected to win, wrote:

> The body is like a bodhi tree,
> And the mind a mirror bright,
> Carefully we wipe them every day
> And let no dust alight.

But an illiterate monk, Hui-neng, asked another monk to write out his poem:

> The body is not like a bodhi tree,
> And there is no mirror bright,
> Since everything is empty to begin with
> Where can the dust alight?

His master immediately saw his depth of understanding and named him his successor.

Sometimes during meditation we in the West can also achieve this awareness. We may call it 'emptiness', and yet it is not a vacuum. White Eagle says in GOLDEN HARVEST,

> When you are confronted with the seeming nothingness which lies beneath the conscious self, you will gradually become aware of an all-ness, a sense of affinity with universal life and at-one-ment with God.

A student in a meditation class I was leading a while ago bears this out. After the meditation, she described how she had always been troubled by a full and busy mind. However, in that meditation she found that she experienced a great emptiness, the absence of mind: but rather than being a nothingness, she said, it was a feeling of deep peace and contentment, of true union with her inner being.

HOW CAN WE BE SIMPLE?

The inspiration for this chapter came very strongly to me after I had been deeply touched by some of White Eagle's words on the simplicity of the masters. The next day I felt impelled to put everything else on one side and just sit down and write. The words just flowed without any struggle, and I felt under a beautiful, clear ray of the star. Then, later, when my writing was typed, I realized there was something missing. I read and re-read what I had written to see if I could add something. I wanted to write about simplicity, but my mind was a blank and nothing flowed! So I showed what I had written to my colleague, Anna, to ask her for any suggestions. What follows is what 'flowed' to her. Simplicity, she considered

—is not being so full of ideas that one cannot listen to others.

—is therefore being open to all life—ready to receive new ideas, ready for change, ready to accept and not to judge others.

—is lack of clutter. It is how you feel when you have spring-cleaned your home and thrown out unwanted accumulations of objects and left-overs, and there is left only one vase of beautiful white blossom on the clear, polished table in the centre of the room: when there is one aspiration alone in one's heart.

—is keeping that one aspiration clearly in mind and letting it alone dictate your life, so that all that is not worthy of it falls away, or into disuse.

—is being one-pointed and humble—seeking no glamour which would again clutter the mind and obscure the heart.

—brings great space in which to expand in tenderness of heart.

—brings the great peace of single-minded devotion.

—is the essence of true strength, because through simplicity of heart, a clear channel is opened to the power of the light.

HOW DO I CULTIVATE SIMPLICITY?

You may think that the achievement of simplicity is easier said than done! Here are some ideas.

1. Keeping your mind clear

When situations are confused, when there is a lot of mental conflict, try to remember the main aspiration of your life on earth. Keep this thought clear in your mind, like a light which cuts through all the surrounding activity and brings you peace.

2. Keeping your heart open

Stay open-hearted to those around you, particularly in difficult situations. Let yourself be vulnerable, take the risk of letting your barriers down; you may appear to be what others call naïve, but never mind. Be trusting, forgiving, generous of spirit, meek, and fearless. Being truly 'vulnerable' and fearless you will live in the present, you will never be downcast and you will always be alive to the goodness and beauty of life.

3. Honesty

Be honest with yourself, and communicate your real feelings to others in a loving way—as children do, but with an adult's understanding and tact!

4. Meditation and visualization

Look at yourself, seeking out anything within your personality and patterns of behaviour which clutters your mind, confuses your emotions or closes and tightens your physical responses. Try to let go of these things. When you are ready to let go of something that has outlived its purpose, you can do this in a number of ways, such as

—meditation (offering it to God in the stillness), or

—visualization (imagining the divine fire in some form consuming and transmuting that which is no longer useful into positive energy).

5. Breathing

In both meditation and visualization, you can use the breath as a tool to help. On the inbreath, draw up out of yourself whatever it is you want to let go. On the outbreath, breathe it out; visualize it melting away in God's healing light.

6. Affirmations

finally, on their own or in conjunction with meditation, visualization and God-breathing, you can cultivate simplicity through affirmation. Here are some specifically on this theme (there are more on the general theme of the chapter on page 112).

I am clear and simple in my thoughts
I let go
I am free to choose in my life
I am free to follow my heart
I am free to flow with God's universe
I am divine simplicity and humility
I am perfect in God.

HUMILITY

The quality of humility goes hand in hand with simplicity, and indeed White Eagle has referred to these qualities as the two pillars through which we pass in order to enter the temple of wisdom. To be humble does not mean that we need to deny our own ability, or put ourselves down, for if we do this, we also 'slay the God within'; sometimes being humble actually means acknowledging our gifts. It means accepting that one is a child of God and that only God knows all and can do all. To be humble means to be able to let go of our own will and of criticism of others, in order to centre our life in God's will. We can work towards this by frequently turning within to listen to God's will, and thus open ourselves more to the inflow of energy from God which enables us to do His will.

WISDOM IS KNOWING THE
RIGHT TIME FOR ANY ACTION

It was only while doing a final revision of the manuscript for this book that I realized I had missed out altogether a crucial aspect of wisdom: timing. Our little selves can be so anxious that we try to do things too soon, or out of fear we leave them too long; maybe we speak too early or too late; maybe we rush through things without due care because of our concern about time; or perhaps we lose all spontaneity because our desire to do things at the right time makes us plan too carefully, allowing no space for God's miracles.

An enlightened soul does none of this. He or she is free to be spontaneous, out of total trust in God and God's timing. This trust allows the energy to flow freely, which means that the moment of every action or non-action is perfectly timed. It is when our natural intuitive impulses are blocked by fear that our action is inappropriate to the moment. Wisdom is the spontaneous choice of action or non-action at exactly the right moment.

CONCLUSION

In conclusion, my advice is that if ever you have difficulty knowing what is the wise thing to do or say, or when to act, just turn within and seek your inner teacher. Here you will eventually find the answer, without fail, for as White Eagle says, 'Your spirit is part of God ... all knowledge lies within you' (p. 59).

THE SIX-POINTED STAR (6)

The way to truth is through the spirit. (p. 60)

 The simple soul empties itself of all preconceived ideas and knowledge and, waiting upon God, becomes as the empty Grail cup.

 When the cup is empty the jewel of true wisdom is revealed. God's light and inspiration fills the waiting heart, and illumines the jewel. God is omniscient—all wisdom.

 The waiting heart is open to God's great wisdom, at one with the flame within the jewel of truth, and able to manifest truth and wisdom in whatever way is needed in the outer life.

A MEDITATION ON 'THE MASTER
SOUL IS WISE IN SPEECH AND ACTION'

*Your spirit is part of God, and all knowledge lies within you. If,
in your meditation, you will go deep within, you will find the centre
of truth and of the infinite powers which await man's use. You will
touch the spring of all happiness and health. (p. 59)*

You are in your innermost sanctuary and your teacher is before
you. As you kneel, he/she offers you a Grail cup. It is very simple
in design, but beautiful in its simplicity. Although it appears
empty, it is radiant with the light.... This is a symbol of how your
teacher wishes you to come forward: in simplicity and humility,
with your consciousness emptied of preconceived views and
judgments, so that you can open yourself to the love and wisdom
of Father–Mother God. Your teacher shows you that at the
bottom of the cup, revealed only when it is empty, lies a beautiful
jewel.

It has many facets which reflect the moving rays of light. He
tells you to watch the jewel, to watch the light, and see how it
gradually becomes very still and the jewel becomes absolutely
clear and sparkling.

Yet this takes a long time; the jewel is so beautiful, it is easy
to become distracted by the reflected light.... Eventually, as you
look deeper and deeper into the jewel, you feel drawn right into
its depths, and there, there at last, is the still, ever-burning flame
of eternal light, love and wisdom ... God.

Meditate here ... allow yourself to become one with the flame
of truth.

111

AFFIRMATIONS (6)

I am wise in speech and action
I am divine wisdom
Not my will, O Lord, but Thy will: show me Thy way
I surrender to God's great love and wisdom
All knowledge lies within me
I am in tune with God's perfect timing
I rest in God's heart. I trust divine wisdom
I am one with God.

7

THE MASTER SOUL IS A TOWER
OF STRENGTH AND LIGHT

Man is spirit—this is all man needs to know: and spirit is triumphant over matter.

TRUE STRENGTH comes from the light within, from God, and thus has the surest possible foundation. We can make the mistake of equating strength or power with domination, but this form of strength comes from the insecurity of the little self and thus has a fatally weak foundation. If we look back into history at the lives of aggressive dictators, it is easy to see how their power was based upon false values and shifting sands. The truly great statesmen have been powerful as a result of their inner strength and the light of wisdom and goodness shining through their actions. Divine strength is also divine gentleness, love, peace and wisdom. Time and again, the lives of spiritual teachers and saints of all time have demonstrated this.

Here is a story about Mohammed, by way of illustration. Mecca (Mohammed's birthplace) had always been a place of pilgrimage, but the people there worshipped many gods and idols, and tried to keep Mohammed and his followers out. One year, the word went round that Mohammed was returning and

113

the people prepared themselves for a battle. But they were amazed to find none of Mohammed's men armed, and instead Mohammed managed to negotiate a peaceful compromise. He then solemnly rode round the city on a white camel, and so impressed the Meccans with his aura of peace and power that they soon allowed him to take over the city and be their ruler.

We do not have to be powerful in the worldly sense of the word in order to be truly strong, nor do we have to be constantly bounding with energy and dynamism. The quiet, gentle soul can be a veritable 'tower of strength', whereas the apparently stronger, more outgoing and ebullient one may go to pieces in a crisis. I had a clear example of this in my own life when there was an emergency just after my son Michael's birth. He collapsed and was in an incubator for three days, and the doctors did not know what was wrong with him. During this time, Madge, my mother-in-law, who was normally a very timid person, became an absolute rock for me, totally steadfast in her conviction that everything would be all right—as indeed it was. Michael had been suffering from the shock of an induced birth and was fine after those first few days.

Madge had revealed her true inner strength, which was usually hidden under a veil of timidity. So it can be with all of us; even if we feel weak on the outside—perhaps because we are conscious of illness in ourselves, or because we are suffering emotional pain or limiting circumstances—we have an unlimited reserve of inner strength and light which we can call upon. We can learn to draw on this when we need it, maybe through the use of affirmations, and always by being steadfast in acknowledging the light in ourselves and developing our awareness of it. True strength does not mean the ability to move physical mountains, to change the world, to lift heavy weights, to run tens of miles or to be an achiever in business; it means to operate always from the spontaneous creativity which comes from being true to our own spiritual nature. We can be bed-ridden and nevertheless be strong. We can be struggling with difficult psychological conditioning and yet be strong. The gentlest person, or one who seems the least intellectual, can be so strong in the light of the spirit within, that their radiance influences everyone around; and of course, the more we do strengthen ourselves in the light, the more the body, mind and outer conditions become harmonious and complete. But this does not usually happen all at once! It seems to be a slow and gradual process which is linked with the whole purpose of life on earth—the spiritualization of matter. But it is an encouraging thought that every effort we make ultimately helps the whole world.

'KEEP ON KEEPING ON'

Sometimes it can be very disheartening if the whole process seems much slower or harder than we feel it should be. I have been working at being strong in a particular situation when the usual reaction of my little self is to crumple like a frightened child at the first sign of apparent disapproval. It is deeply ingrained in my little self to want the approval of certain authority figures, and I still find it hard, on occasions, to be strong in the light of my own inner guidance. It seems to be a very long, ongoing process, but every time I succeed in being strong when I need to be, I feel I have achieved a step forward, even if I cannot maintain it all the time.

I expect we all have days when we feel more than usually weak and cut off from the light. This can be particularly true if we are struggling with illness. Recently my mother, Joan Hodgson, has suffered much physical pain, first through a badly-shattered elbow, and latterly through the illness shingles. Hard though these experiences have been, she has told me that she would not have wanted them taken from her, for she is conscious of what she has learnt through her suffering and she feels more able to understand the difficulty of the many patients who write to her for healing help. She has experienced at first hand the struggle to be 'strong in the light' while coping with great pain and debilitating illness, as well as the necessity for surrender and the magical release that learning to 'bow into the pain' can bring. She has found how much it *does* help steadfastly to keep on keeping on, calling on the inner light to arise. *I am the resurrection and the life* is a very powerful affirmation for these times.

It is helpful to remember that no condition is hopeless. God, the God within our own being, is all-powerful and can even re-create tissue and living cells. White Eagle teaches us that the more we learn to 'sound the note of God', by which he means the keynote of love, clearly and in all we think and do, the more easily can the miraculous power of the light heal our bodies and give us the strength to transform our lives. 'Basically all healing is the intake into the body of the eternal Sun, the Light,' says White Eagle (p. 73). 'If you can call upon this Light, breathe it in, live consciously in this Light, it will actually control the cells of the physical body.'

Yet, if you find this very difficult to do right now, if you are feeling heavy and weighed down, if your body is sick and your life seems hard, do not blame yourself. Incarnation in matter is often far from easy and sometimes we just have to trust that the light really *is* still shining, however hidden, and that things *will* change. Many present-day illnesses are an expression, and an outworking, at the physical level, of very deep karmic situations;

it is worth remembering, though, that they also reflect the deliberate choice of growth-experience, something which can best be learned through ill-health. I believe a soul has the opportunity before each incarnation to choose from certain possibilities for the next life. A major disability or illness may be one of the options, and accepting this is always the freewill choice of the soul concerned. What is chosen is not necessarily past-life karma; it may be an entirely fresh opportunity for which the soul has now sufficient strength.

Some conditions, however, are created by ourselves in this day of life, and although it may appear outwardly that we have caught a virus, or there is some other source that can be blamed, all disease is actually created by ourselves out of our own disharmony. Its origin is not 'out there', but inside ourselves. The miracle is that the power to heal all disease also lies within ourselves; and that power, of course, is the light of God.

Here, verbatim, is a brave comment from a friend who has suffered much through physical illness in recent years:

> I would really appreciate some healing love at this time. I expect they will operate on the Friday, and I know some healing prayers will strengthen and inspire my courage, which at moments like this can, of one's self, seem very small.
>
> I know I am given so much help with the healing I am receiving already, for though the physical difficulties continue I know I am strengthened in spirit, and so often aware of the comfort and support of the healing angels and our brothers in spirit who aid us in our faltering steps upon the path.

Whatever is going on in our lives, however hard our path, it is reassuring to remember that no effort to arise in spirit is ever wasted. The effort in itself is a form of service to all life. As we read in chapter five, 'If you endeavour to raise the Christ within you, you help to raise all mankind' (p. 53). Indeed, a call to the aspiring spirit within could be one interpretation of Jesus's words in St Luke's gospel: *I say unto thee, Arise, and take up thy couch, and go into thine house.*

WINGS OF LIGHT

In our healing services in the White Eagle Lodge, we use some words of White Eagle's about 'rising as on wings of light into the heavenly state, into the very heart of the Sun'. This powerful and helpful image is also contained in the symbolism of the winged disc. When the first White Temple was planned, for the hilltop at New Lands, White Eagle gave specific instructions that this ancient symbol be placed above the entrance, just as it is seen, even to this day, over all the portals in the Egyptian temples. For me, seeing the symbol is a constant reminder of mankind's ability to rise 'as on wings of light' out of heavy earthiness into the spiritual light.

A few years ago I had an experience in meditation which helped me realize that I had the choice whether to rise on wings of light or whether to allow myself to feel heavy and burdened. In my meditation I was taking part in a ceremony of joyous celebration just before I reincarnated. Many friends had gathered to join in what seemed to be a 'birthday party'! I am sure there are many such celebrations for incoming souls. It was a spontaneous, light-hearted occasion and everyone was dancing and singing. We sometimes think of spiritual celebrations in the world of light as always being serious affairs, but White Eagle assures us they are not. Holiness is 'whole-ness' and wholeness is joyful. As the celebration was drawing to a close, I felt my teacher tell me that an important part of my task for this incarnation was to bring this joyous 'light-heartedness' into all my work and give the gift of joy and a light heart to all those who were drawn into work and play with me.

Since this memory came back, I have often thought about joy and ways to create more light-heartedness and fun. It seems to me that joy is inextricably linked to the well of creativity that is naturally within us all, within all our hearts. It is as natural to life as is breathing, and just as essential to our health and well-being. It is like a spring of clear water bubbling up spontaneously from the mountainside, and helps us see our whole world with new eyes and with a sense of wonder and thankfulness for the glory of God's creation. I think God means our life to be joyful and filled with happiness, not heavy and burdensome. Joy is more complete than 'pleasure' because joy is a total experience which embraces the whole self—that is, joy is of body, soul and spirit rather than merely of the body, or the mind, or the emotions. Ultimately all joy comes from God. Usually, I think, it takes many lifetimes of searching, temporary fulfilment, disillusionment and more searching (a 'path' which is so clearly illustrated in the story of Siddhartha's life) before we can finally centre ourselves in the divine joy which comes from loving God and serving God in man.

WHAT GETS IN THE WAY OF JOY?

One day I realized how often I was unnecessarily shutting out joy. I was at the start of a particularly busy day, and in my mind I was worrying about how I could manage to get through everything, and feeling that I was under great pressure. I was cooking lunch for our guests arriving on retreat and was heaving a pan of potatoes into the oven, feeling very weak and tired as I did it. Suddenly I felt the spirit form of my grandmother, Minesta, at my side. She laughed and said, 'Take it lightly, dear. Just dance through the day and have fun wherever you can.' Her words totally transformed that day for me. I could not literally dance, but I did have a feeling of light-heartedness, and from that moment everything seemed to go much more smoothly. Recently I came across these words of White Eagle's:

> We often think that you do not dance sufficiently. You do not dance in your hearts, in your minds, in your bodies. We see the fairies always moving in rhythm and dancing and using the colours of the etheric world to build most beautiful temple homes. We would like to see all our brethren full of the joy of the universal love.

One of the factors which may serve to dampen our feeling of joy in life is failure to provide time which is just for ourselves; time to do things which we really enjoy and are not just done to please others. Doing things for others promotes great joy, of course, but to be too caught up in caring—a very common situation for many working mothers, for instance—can be a reason for feeling joyless and heavy-hearted. It can also be a cause of resentment building up inside ourselves, only to burst out later in ways that others call inappropriate and unhelpful.

Another reason for joy dying is that we feel trapped in a difficult situation we feel unable to change. It is this feeling of powerlessness, in particular, which stifles joy, because joy and empowerment are so closely linked. We feel joyful when we are in touch with the God within, with the source of all creativity, and this very creativity is what can bring about change. So in a situation where we feel powerless we need to look at what we can do to acknowledge our inner power. It may not be possible at the time to change the outer conditions, but we can change *inside* (for we always have the freedom and power to do this) and thus put ourselves back in touch with the joy which is to be found in any and every situation. Here again, affirmations can be very helpful. You might choose one like *My life is filled with love and joy*, or *My life is fun: miracles are happening all the time in my life*.

Something else which can stifle joy is the continual denial of our abilities, so that we never give ourselves the chance to be fulfilled and creative. Typically, we give others the power to be the judge of our worth in some way, and then when they seem to put us down, it causes us to lose faith in ourselves. For example, I have a friend who is a talented artist, but she finds it hard to believe in herself because her father was a perfectionist with strong views about art. I encourage her to try to have faith in herself and her own unique gift, even if its execution is very different from her father's.

So, if you doubt your own ability because, maybe, you are different from how your parents or how someone else thinks you should be, please believe in yourself and trust in *your own* guidance, not theirs. Never let others deny the perfection in you. Get rid of the 'parrot on the shoulder' telling you what you should or shouldn't do, and be free to be yourself. You are a unique and wonderful human being, and with God's love and creativity flowing freely through you, you can do *anything*!

THE SIX-POINTED STAR (7)

The Christ within you is King ... every particle, every cell of your body, is subject to the divine power and glory. Realize the divine magical presence within you. The Light overcomes all darkness. (p. 69)

The upward-pointing triangle stands for the soul aspiring to the light, and working to keep the spontaneous joy flowing freely from the heart to embrace all life. This joy increasingly allows true power and strength to manifest.

'You keep yourself in bondage, in chains!', says White Eagle. 'Throw off the chains of this earthly darkness and see yourself as you truly are....' (p. 67)

Realize the divine magical presence within you—the downward-pointing triangle. When the soul makes this effort, it opens the path for magical happenings. When love and joy are affirmed, love, strength, joy and healing flood the heart and the life. 'Every atom, every cell of your body will be filled with perfect life.' (pp. 69, 75)

The star represents a soul in incarnation in a physical body, but transformed, illumined, joyous and light-filled ... a tower of strength and light.

A MEDITATION ON 'THE MASTER
SOUL IS A TOWER OF STRENGTH AND LIGHT'

See yourself as you truly are, a son–daughter of the blazing, golden Light of the Sun. (p. 67)

Visualize yourself standing under a beautiful fountain of clear and refreshing healing water. This spiritual water is composed of healing light, and so it does not make you at all wet, but it does wash away all the heaviness of earth, all earthly problems and sickness.

Allow your visualization to take whatever form is right for you. For example, you may see yourself first of all dressed in heavy dark clothes or armour, and then the clear healing water starts gently falling on you, until you stand open to the light, clothed in simple garments of light.

Now, healed and cleansed, you feel light-hearted and illumined by joy surging up within; and as you face your teacher, you see that he or she is light-hearted too. Divine power and strength flow through every cell of your body. You know that with this strength you can do anything God asks of you.

Together with your teacher you set out on a joyous adventure. Maybe your visualization will lead you now to fly, your teacher beside you, on a beautiful white bird or winged horse, to a heavenly place of light and joyous celebration; or maybe you will be sent forth with a special task to perform ... which you know you can fulfil, for you are a tower of strength and light.

123

AFFIRMATIONS (7)

I am a tower of strength and light
*Divine light shines in me: I am divine light. Divine life permeates
and heals every atom of my being.* I am *the resurrection and the life*
I am one with the infinite Sun
I am a radiant child of God
I am divine joy
I am divine creativity
I can do anything
My life is filled with love and joy
My life is fun: miracles are happening all the time in my life.

8

THE MASTER SOUL
BEARS NO RESENTMENT

Nothing happens out of order or by chance, and the great Law brings those very conditions in your life which you need for growth. So accept with love all that happens.

THERE IS a Zen koan (one of those extraordinary paradoxical statements in Zen which unlocks the mind from its usual patterns) which asks, 'What is the sound of one hand clapping?' Sometimes it is hard to grasp with our everyday minds the full significance of what White Eagle is really saying. Like the author of the Zen koan, he has a way of expressing something profound in such a simple way that it is possible to overlook the depth of its meaning. Perhaps after years of contemplation, we may find that a sentence of his brings enlightenment in a flash.

One of the things he tells us is 'Nothing happens by chance'. If you spend time contemplating what this really means, its implications in our daily lives are astounding. While preparing this book I came across a newspaper article on the subject of coincidences. It quoted an extraordinary story of someone who felt impelled to pull the emergency cord on an underground train at the very moment that someone else (totally unconnectedly) was attempting suicide by throwing himself in front of the train. The suicide attempt failed simply because of the seemingly unrelated action on the other person's part.

I think most people have stories to tell, though perhaps not as spectacular as this, of coincidences which have occurred in their lives which have proved to be remarkably significant. For example, a 'chance' meeting with a long-lost acquaintance which led to a renewal of a deep friendship. Sometimes these incidents, which seem to happen by chance, appear truly miraculous, but in fact they are all a beautiful outworking of God's law of life. In the well-known book A COURSE IN MIRACLES, we read:

> Miracles occur naturally as expressions of love. The real miracle is the love that inspires them.... There is no order of difficulty in miracles. One is not 'harder' or 'bigger' than another. They are all the same. All expressions of love are maximal.*

On the subject of miracles, I love White Eagle's words (in an unpublished teaching), 'The star is a creator of miracles.' Many people have told of the remarkable way in which the symbol of the star has helped them in moments of crisis, and indeed prompted a so-called miracle. I quote from a letter received a few years ago.

> I must tell you about the miracle which has happened in my life. I had just been diagnosed as having cancer and was in a state of shock, when I felt guided to go into a second-hand bookshop. Seemingly 'by chance' the first book I picked up was HEAL THYSELF. This seemed very appropriate and I was immediately drawn to the six-pointed star on its cover. I can truthfully say that book has proved a turning-point in my life.

*A COURSE IN MIRACLES, vol. 1, chapter 1, page 1 (Penguin Books, London, 1978)

I read it from cover to cover (and then sent for more White Eagle books) and I tried really to live what White Eagle was saying. I realized that my cancer was an opportunity for me to take stock of my life and make a new start. Every day I used the affirmation given in the book, '*I am* the star; the light of the eternal fires radiates through me and *is* the star.' I felt this glorious light truly radiating through every cell of my body, cleaning away all the cancer and all the negative emotion which I felt had caused it in the first place. I felt a new person, and believed that a miracle really had happened in my life. When I returned to the specialist he was amazed, because the follow-up tests at the hospital revealed no trace of cancer in my body at all.

In another letter, a member of the White Eagle Lodge wrote about the way using the star in her daily meditations had transformed *her* life:

I am so thankful for the inner prompting which led me to come along to the London Lodge. Almost by chance it seemed I found myself with a few hours to spare, and I decided on the spur of the moment to attend a healing service. I never looked back. The star changed everything for me. My illness, the questions and bitterness, are all behind me. At last I am at peace, and every second of the day fills my heart with joy and the love of God!

The saying at the head of this chapter continues: 'Accept with love all that happens. Look for the lesson that has to be learnt from the experience.' Herein White Eagle gives us a clear pointer to help us in our growth. He tells us there is a lesson in even the most trying and testing circumstances. Sometimes the lesson is very clear, at other times rather obscure. In the first letter, my correspondent clearly saw that the reason for her cancer was to give her an opportunity to cleanse herself of all the negative emotions stored up inside her. But often we cannot immediately see the deeper reasons behind what is happening. I don't think this matters. In fact, I believe that it is not the knowing which is significant, but rather the deeper conviction and faith that nothing does happen by chance. White Eagle's teaching tells us*:

Life is law. This law governs life, from the smallest detail to the greatest—to the Universe itself. So if chance appears to bring 'luck', remember that it is the result of a law which you yourself have set in motion....

Law—that is the answer to all doubting and questioning. Law—undeviating, never erring, never hasting, never forgetting, never failing. Law—so precise, so exact that it makes due allowance for that which man calls his freewill, much as the engineer allows play for each bearing. Law—which is perfect justice, unfailing wisdom, yet so merciful that it lays no burden on any man beyond his strength, which takes full account of frailty, yet eventually constrains each soul to the full exercise of its powers, under the spur and penalty of suffering. Law—which while it exacts to the last farthing, never fails to recompense or to return full measure, pressed down and running over. Law—which beyond the understanding of the outer mind, beyond all dreams, hope and prayers, proves to be love, patience, forbearance and compassion for each and every man.

ACCEPTING THE LAW WITH LOVE

If we can come totally to believe what White Eagle is telling us, the lesson of acceptance will come much more easily for us, for

*In the White Eagle magazines STELLA POLARIS, vol. IX, p. 65, and ANGELUS, 1937, p.150

we will know without question that all life is governed by this wonderful and miraculous law, and planned upon a grand computer which never makes mistakes.

I have found that truly accepting that nothing happens by chance and that there is a lesson in everything has helped me to flow with things as they are and trust in God. It has also helped me to consider that the happening might be a signal that there is something in the pattern of my life which needs looking at and possibly that a change needs to be made. To use a trivial example, I lost my contact lens twice within a short space of time and I took this as a reminder that I needed to go back to the optician for a check-up. Sure enough, this did prove to be quite significant, because the optician suggested some improved lenses which would be much better in the long term for my eyes.

The 'nothing happens by chance' theme is even more significant, of course, in the major issues of our lives. Losing our job, or finding ourselves in a very difficult relationship situation, for instance, are not just the result of some unfair turn of fate. They are either new opportunities for learning and growing, or karmic debts which, in our higher selves, we have chosen to repay at this particular moment. Our little self may complain how unfair life is, but our true self knows better. Our teacher knows better too, and he or she is always ready to help and support us, and lift us above the pain and confusion while we are learning the necessary lessons. For White Eagle tells us that our karma is really about unlearned lessons. Sometimes we *do* have a choice and can make constructive outer changes in our lives, but at other times the only option we have is to accept our debts and do our best to learn the lesson, because once we have done this the difficult karma will no longer exist.

A friend of mine was made redundant a few years ago. The

redundancy was very unexpected and it came as a great shock to him. There was nothing he could do to change the situation and he had to look for another job. As for so many people, this was very hard and everything he tried proved to be a dead end. After a while, during which he felt very depressed, asking only resentfully, 'Why should this have happened to me?', he started really to look for the answer to that question. Each day when his wife and children had left for work and school, instead of wandering around the house in his dressing gown, feeling angry or sad that he no longer had a reason to be up and dressed and going out himself, he decided to do something positive. He chose to get himself ready at the usual time, as if preparing for work, but not to make a physical journey, out of the house to a place of work, but a journey inwards to find God. Whereas before he had never had the time, or so he thought, to meditate regularly, he suddenly realized that he no longer had that excuse and he would make the first 'job' of each day his hour of meditation.

He made a quiet place in his bedroom where he could sit comfortably in front of a beautiful picture that really inspired him, and he also lit a candle. He was not at all experienced at meditation, but he decided to use a section of the White Eagle book THE STILL VOICE each day. At first it was very hard indeed and he was sure he was 'getting nowhere', but he persevered and gradually realized how it was transforming his day. He had more energy and was able to think clearly and constructively about his whole life. He understood many things about his life and the realization totally transformed him; and he came to see the wonderful gift his redundancy had been. Once he had come to this point, he found new work and everything opened up for him.

This is a good example of what White Eagle teaches us about acceptance. If we can truly accept what has happened in our lives and let the past go, then there is space for God's beautiful plan to unfold in our lives. It is our letting go which creates the space, and this is much easier to do if we trust absolutely that what has happened is for our ultimate good and will save us more pain in the long run. Often, on looking back, it is possible to see things in a different perspective and recognize the beautiful gift hidden in the aftermath of the upset, and to realize at last how God has already brought something more beautiful into our life.

ACCEPTANCE CAN MEAN POSITIVELY EMBRACING A CHALLENGE!

The story of my friend who was made redundant is a helpful example in another way too, because it shows that to accept with love all that happens does not mean a weak and hopeless resignation to it, but rather a positive embracing of a challenge. When White Eagle tells us to renounce things, he does not mean us to become weak and feeble puppets of fate. He means that we need to let go of our limited perception of how things ought to be, or how we wish them to be. For example, 'I want to keep that job.... I must keep that job....' in the face of unavoidable redundancy; or 'I want my lover back.... It is so unfair that he/she left me for so-and-so.'

When we can break free from our limited perception, we open our eyes and become aware of a wider perspective which reveals new opportunities. My friend was able to overcome his feelings of despondency and hopelessness and embrace the new opportunity. This new opportunity came in the unexpected package of an inner journey to work, rather than an outer one. Opportunities often do come wrapped up in unexpected packages, as I mentioned earlier. I think we need to take care that we do not throw away the opportunity because its outer covering looks unattractive, or not exactly what we had expected or wanted!

This was illustrated very clearly for me in a story I heard my aunt tell many years ago. She told how her mother had offered her a jewel box as a gift. It was rather shabby and not what she really wanted. She responded, 'Oh, I don't want that old thing!' Her mother cautioned her not to be so hasty, and to look inside. When she did this, she found a beautiful brooch. It was the very brooch she had always wanted, and she had almost refused it! This story made a deep impression on me. So don't refuse unexpected opportunities, for they may contain the very 'jewel' for which you have always longed.

One part of the lesson of acceptance can be about bravely taking on a new challenge; and another part about being able to let go the past and allow things to be as they are. In chapter four, I wrote about the positive and negative (masculine and feminine) aspects of peace. I think acceptance has this dual aspect, too: the quiet feminine surrender to the greater will of God, but also the positive masculine embrace of the new opportunity, bringing change and challenge.

White Eagle tells us that 'the master soul bears no resentment', and one way in which we can help ourselves towards this often-difficult goal is to become clearer about the things we can change and the things we cannot. I have found this well-known prayer most helpful:

> God grant me the serenity to accept the things
> I cannot change,
> The courage to change the things I can,
> And the wisdom to know the difference.

When we come up against things in our relationships which we cannot change, White Eagle's teaching helps us to flow with things as they are, and accept the wisdom of God's plan for our lives; but there are also times when it is possible to take practical action which will greatly relieve a trying situation. Sometimes all that is required is the courage lovingly to tell the other person how one feels, and ask for their help in making it better. This always works better than blaming the other person for creating the problem! If the situation is more complicated than this, it can be amazing how prayer and asking for help at an inner level gradually transform things.

Here is an example. A colleague told me how resentful she had been feeling about her husband not getting on with things. She felt very stuck in the situation, and could see that nagging and complaining was not helping, but she couldn't stop herself because she wanted things done which she couldn't do herself. She could see her husband found her difficult to be with, and that he was withdrawing even more.

In the end she simply sat down and tried to let go of the negative feelings, without much success, because she kept remembering yet another little thing which hadn't been done. That day, in sheer desperation, she asked White Eagle to help her let go of the negative feelings—and it worked. Before long she felt calmer, and when her husband came home she was able to smile and accept him for how he was. Miraculously, from that moment, things started to change. He began to get things done and even people outside the family offered to help, without her saying anything about the situation at all!

Timing is often very significant in things like this. Usually we want change to happen immediately. I certainly do, and yet I have found it helpful to remember that there is 'an acceptable time of the Lord'. If your prayers don't seem to be answered and the difficult situation just goes on ... and on ... trust that the miracle can and will happen—at the right moment.

We are often tempted also to feel that we have to 'stand up for our rights', but White Eagle teaches that 'God adjusts things with exact law'. In order to see how this can be we often have to take a long view, to change our perspective. I once wrote a magazine article entitled, 'How things look all depends on where you are when you are looking at them!' The more emotionally involved we are in a situation, the more difficult it can be to detach ourselves sufficiently to see clearly. Here again, affirmations can be a very powerful tool to help us let go of strong feelings and become more balanced and centred. As our emotions calm down, it becomes easier to trust in God's infinite wisdom and justice and perhaps even to see how all the pieces of God's giant jigsaw may ultimately fit together.

THE SIX-POINTED STAR (8)

God holds the plan, my dear one, always God holds the plan, so when things do not go according to your plan, remember, do not fuss, just fit in. This doesn't mean letting go your responsibilities. It means that when you have done all you can according to your power, the rest is in God's hands. Take your mortal hands off, and let God work His will. (p. 82)

The upward-pointing triangle represents the soul aspiring to be guided at all times by the light of God within, and always to do the best it can, however testing the circumstances.

Our aspiration opens the channel for the light we need, and for the inspiration from our teacher—represented by the symbol of the downward-pointing triangle. This inspiration helps us have the courage to act and to know when is the best time to act. It also helps us feel intuitively when we need to be still and wait quietly for the plan for our lives to unfold.

The star stands for the soul who has integrated the two ways of being; the way of wise action and the way of quiet waiting. It symbolizes the soul who can embrace, at appropriate moments, both the way of courageous action leading to new growth and joy, and the way of peaceful acceptance of things as they are. In the star-consciousness, we know God's plan is perfect.

A MEDITATION ON 'THE MASTER SOUL BEARS NO RESENTMENT'

There is so much which you cannot understand in human relationship; often you have to endure what seems to be injustice. But those in the spirit world, who can take the long view, can always tell you that all crooked places will be made straight and all injustice will be righted. (p. 80)

In your imagination feel that you are being lifted up, as on wings of light, to a place far above the everyday world. All around you snow-covered mountain peaks are sparkling in the sunshine. You find yourself sitting on a plateau of soft grass, yet surrounded by the mountains. It is not cold, but the air is very crisp and clean, and it seems easy to feel the presence of your teacher and other brothers of the light.

There is a feeling of timelessness and eternity. There is no fret and hurry here ... no restless pacing. All is still, except for the gentle perambulation in rhythm with the great *Aum, Aum, Aum,* the heartbeat of God and all life. Consciously attune yourself to this gentle rhythm, and feel God's love and light flow through your whole being, bringing you deep peace and acceptance. All the problems of your earthly life can fade into insignificance here, for here all things assist you in taking the long view ... and you can open your heart totally to God's love and the beauty of His plan for your life and the life of all humanity.

136

AFFIRMATIONS (8)

I bear no resentment: nothing happens out of order or by chance
The great Law brings these very conditions into my life so that I may grow
I accept with love all that happens
I trust in the divine plan
I trust God's infinite wisdom
I trust God's timing
I have the courage to change the things I can. I have the serenity to accept what I cannot change. I have the wisdom to know the difference
I have the courage to move forward at the acceptable time of the Lord
I let go. I accept. I trust
I am in God and God is in me.

9

THE MASTER SOUL IS PATIENT, TRUSTING IN GOD'S GOODNESS AND HIS PERFECT PLAN

It is because you cannot see far enough along the road your spirit must travel that you become overwrought with fear and anxiety.

FEAR IS ONE of the greatest challenges which faces us, and it is one of the things I would most like to be able to let go of in myself. 'Fear and doubts too long have bound us: Free our hearts to work and praise', go the words of a well-known hymn. Fears and doubts so often *do* bind us, and we seem to spend much of our lives burdened by fear. White Eagle and many other spiritual teachers assure us that we have no need to fear, and that we can put our trust in God and His plan for our own lives. I have been brought up with these ideals. I know them with my mind and I do trust in God, but even so, I find my little self is often fearful. I have thought about this often in recent years, and I have come to the conclusion that feeling fear is a very valuable part of our spiritual growth and that if it were magically taken away from us, like any of our karma, our souls would be denied many opportunities to expand and learn. I know that in my own inner growth in recent years, the fact that I have felt many fears, and in some cases been able to 'go through them', has been of great value to me. White Eagle talks of the law of compensation, and I have found at first hand how this works. Each time I have faced a fear and 'gone through it', the wonderful compensation has been the increased inner joy and security I have felt as I became more aware of God's enfolding love and care for me. Here is an illustration.

I had been facing a fear of breaking down in my car when driving alone. One day I had arranged to meet a friend some distance away. At the last minute I telephoned to arrange a different meeting place; because it was such a sunny day, a country rendezvous seemed more appealing than the town. Thus my journey involved a drive on twisting roads, rather than a fast motorway, and so of necessity I went slowly. As I drove I had an increasing inner awareness that something was wrong with my car, but I didn't know what. I arrived safely, however, and had a lovely day out with my friend.

I had tried to put the fear about my car out of my mind during the day, but as I drove home it became increasingly apparent that there really was something wrong. As I drove, I prayed that I would be helped to get home ('I trust in God', I kept saying) and I felt a wonderful reassurance from my teacher. By now it was the evening rush-hour and as I came to a traffic jam at a large roundabout some people leaned out of their car and shouted, 'Your wheel is about to drop off!' I was terrified, but almost the next moment I noticed a large Ford garage (my car was a Ford) immediately opposite me. I managed to drive slowly into it; by now it was six o'clock, and a Friday evening, and I was lucky to find someone at the reception, but they said it was too late to do anything. I would have to leave my car there and make my own way home. I did not know how, as I was still many miles away and there was no public transport. As I walked away, two men appeared from the back of the garage and said, 'Can we help you, love?'

I told them what had happened and they immediately looked at my wheel, sorted out the problem, said, 'No, you don't owe us anything', and disappeared! I drove home safely with my heart full of thanksgiving to God for His wonderful care of me.

If I had not changed my plan and driven on slow roads, I should probably have been killed, as my wheel had all its nuts loose and would certainly have flown off at high speed. Looking back on it, I realize that this incident had an even deeper significance for me, because the increased trust in God it brought me enabled me to make a major change in my personal life for which I had needed the courage for some time.

This story has a sequel. Later, the mechanic responsible for leaving the nuts loose on my car came to apologize. 'You must be very angry with me for being so careless and putting your life at risk,' he said. When I replied, 'No, I am thanking you because it has helped me trust in God's care for me even more!', he was very startled and said, 'Well, now I must thank God and trust Him more too!'

OUR WORST FEARS USUALLY NEVER HAPPEN

Many of the things we fear never actually happen. One thing that can make us fearful is an over-active imagination stimulated by the negativity which seems to be all around us in society. This negative energy is not necessarily bad, for negativity can stimulate growth and deeper compassion, but too much of it can be destructive. The media coverage of news can exaggerate situations and quite wrongly increase our fears. I was very aware of this when I was preparing for a journey to Turkey which had been booked before the Gulf war broke out. As the date of my departure grew near, people all around me were deciding it was not safe to travel anywhere, and I felt very affected by the general atmosphere of fear. I would certainly have cancelled my plans if it had not been for my inner conviction that my plans had to go ahead and that I would be looked after. White Eagle's guidance came so clearly as I opened THE QUIET MIND one morning and read:

> Never fear your journey ahead, for as God has watched over you all your life and, in spite of your fears, has brought you through all the trials and sorrows of your life, so He will take you through the darkest vale, into the light. (p. 94)

His reassurance was absolutely right, because my journey was without incident and I felt further away from the war than those at home, who were continually bombarded by news bulletins.

I had a clear demonstration of how the media do exaggerate a situationwhen two days before I set off the television news showed pictures of soldiers and tanks at Heathrow airport (there were fears of terrorist attacks) and I expected it to look very different from usual, but when I was there I saw no sign of the army at all, and everything was quiet.

A smaller example occurred more recently when I was due to make a winter nighttime drive alone, and a colleague came into my office and advised me not to risk it because the fog was so bad. I could see for myself how bad the fog was, and my fear increased enormously. However, I very much wanted to make the journey and my inner guidance told me to have the courage to go ahead because I would not find it so bad after all. So I set out feeling very apprehensive but determined, and after about five miles a miracle happened, as the fog suddenly dispersed and it became a clear, starry night. I completed my journey quickly and safely.

Because our thoughts are so powerful, I believe that if we expect negative conditions we are much more likely to attract them into our lives than if we expect positive, safe and loving happenings. So one way in which we can work to let go our fear is by being very positive and optimistic and not allowing ourselves to be pulled down by the fears of others.

The 'Emmanuel' books, which are full of teaching extremely similar in feeling to White Eagle's, contain a very helpful statement about fear*:

> Every moment of your life
> you are offered the opportunity to choose—
> love or fear,
> to tread the earth
> or to soar the heavens.

And this is it. We either fear, or love. So when we apply that distinction to individual situations, we find we really do have a choice. In answer to the question, 'How can we stop worrying about the ones we love?', Emmanuel continues:

> By trusting
> the absolute wisdom of each soul.
> Worry is distrust
> put into a slot
> that seems socially acceptable.
> If you say,
> 'I am worried about the children',
> everyone says, 'Yes, of course',
> and thinks you are a good parent.
> But if you should say,

*See EMMANUEL'S BOOK and EMMANUEL'S BOOK II (Bantam Books, New York, 1985 and 1989)

'I really don't trust the Divine Plan',
what do you think the reaction would be?
This leads us to the principal statement which both teachers are making. In the words of the Bible, *'Perfect love casteth out fear.'*

LOVE OVERCOMES FEAR

In another passage, Emmanuel says: 'Fear is the frightened child. Love is the flame of holy remembering.'

Love is the great antidote to fear. If we can project love into the situation we are in, it *always* helps. White Eagle would say that this is divine Law. If we can attempt to love the people or the conditions involved because they are teaching us, then fear dissolves. The love we feel cancels out the fear and fills the mind with joy, so that fear can't get in any more. I remember my aunt telling the story of how her mother, Grace Cooke, had helped her when she was feeling fearful about standing up in front of a large group of people to conduct a service and give a talk for the first time. My grandmother had said, 'Just stand up there and love them, dear.'

This has helped me on similar occasions, and on reading this chapter in its draft form, Anna too said to me: 'Just remembering this has helped me face many of the public situations I have found myself in over the last few months. When I feel love towards the people who are waiting for me to speak, it changes entirely how I feel about the situation. I am no longer thinking about what I am doing and worrying about it. I am thinking of them and their well-being, and thinking of how I can make what I say appropriate for them and relevant and how I can set them at their ease, rather than being at ease myself. I feel that this typifies again the emphasis that we place on the work that we do on ourselves.

If we put others first, and the spirit first above all, we ourselves also gain immeasurably from our effort.'

I have found it helpful to try to get into the way of replacing any negative thought with a positive one. As soon as I realize that a negative, fearful thought has taken a grip of my mind, I try to think of all the examples of God's care for me I have already experienced. By an act of choice—really, by acting on the will of our true selves—I think that we can change our fear thoughts into positive or even thankful ones instead. Fears often come about when we are thinking of a future possibility and imagine an outcome in which we feel that we would be unable to cope. We fear that we will be running out of control and helpless. A way to correct that feeling is to realize that God is in control: and then to realize that this also means the part of God which is inside *us*.

Be here now—an antidote to fear

We are never asked to cope with more than we can handle, and always the strength is there when we need it, White Eagle says. It is the fear of not coping, and the fear of fear itself, which often paralyses us, or makes us panic. It is the thought that everything is going to get worse, rather than about what *is*. So, it helps very much if we can guide our thoughts to the present moment only, and into the feeling of God's love upholding us, in this moment of now and for all time. Live as much as you can in this moment. It will help so much if you work to stay centred in the present and do not allow your mind to travel off into dire fantasies of what might be.

Exercises in concentration are a help in this. For example, practise until you are able to concentrate your attention totally on the still flame, or the star, for five minutes at a time, not just once, but regularly. This is particularly helpful if you are prone to panic attacks or phobias, to sleeplessness or mental agitation. If your fear is exacerbated by a sensitive nervous system, then a diet which does not involve too many stimulants, and a lifestyle in which your inner sensitivity is balanced by strong 'outward' activities such as gardening, walking in nature, sport, things which 'earth' you, also help.

MAKING THE MOST OF THE OPPORTUNITY OUR FEARS BRING!

1. Unrecognized fears

Quite often our fear is of a rather general nature and we are not really sure what the fear is all about. We may feel uncomfortable and anxious inside, without being quite sure why. The primitive human reaction to fear is to want to run away, or push it away into a dark recess of the mind, hoping, maybe, that when we next look, the fear will have gone away. Sadly this is not usually the case! If we have the courage to look at our fears and let the light shine on them, they can give us their gift, which is the opportunity to grow stronger in our love for God, and in our trust of the incredible, intricate beauty of the mosaic He has designed for our unfoldment.

If your fear is of a general, unspecific nature, it can be helpful to work on it with an affirmation on the theme of letting go fear and trusting in God, such as *I .... (insert your name) let go all fear. I trust in God and in His perfect plan for my life* or *I am strong in the light of the star.*

As these affirmations begin to remind you of your inner strength, you can start to look further into the nature of your fear. Try asking your body and your body-mind what it is afraid of. The best time to do this is when you are relaxing in bed, during yoga relaxation, or after quietly attuning yourself to the inner light through slow, deep breathing. As you breathe quietly and gently and focus all your attention inwards, say something like, 'Dear "little self", I love you and am doing my best to care for you. God loves you and always ensures that the best happens for you. Tell me what is the matter. What do you fear?

Then just stop and listen to yourself. Try to put aside all your rational thoughts and not to shut out the spontaneous answer which will pop up from somewhere inside you. If nothing comes, leave it. Don't try to force anything, or rationalize an answer. On another occasion, when the time is right, it will come, or if it doesn't, it may be that using the general affirmation has melted the fear away anyway. I was greatly helped by a book called FOCUSING by Eugene Gendlin,* which provides a very helpful and gentle technique for becoming clearer about the nature of our fears, so that we can then do something positive about them.

2. When you know what your fear is

If you know what your fear is, don't push it away and tell yourself how silly you are. Accept that this is how it is, and give your little self some love. It can be very helpful to use visualization to help let go of fear; for example you could imagine wrapping the fear up in a parcel and burning it, or see it as being like a bundle you carry on your back and which you take off and leave behind.

Sometimes it is helpful to look at a past incident in our lives which seemed like an absolute disaster, and yet everything turned out well after all. The realization and remembrance of this helps trust to grow stronger, as I found after my experience with the wheel nearly coming off my car. You may also find, as I did, that certain very important things resulted which could not have

*Published by Bantam Books, New York

taken place otherwise. The way was cleared for them. It does also help to say 'Thank you God'! The very act of saying thank you—especially if done out loud—actually releases something inside and helps us assimilate the lessons more easily. I have found that looking back in positive remembrance, in a sort of ritual of completion, is a vital stepping-stone towards helping me have the confidence to move forward through any new fear.

3. Working with small fears

Our work to move through fear can be as much over little things as over the major ones. Here is an example from my own life which I thought trivial at first, but which I now see as quite significant for me. I love fun-fairs, and over the last few years, since I have been consciously working on fear, I have become more bold about the rides I go on. However, until recently I had never gone on the bumper cars as I thought they were too rough for me, and the jolts would be too much. On one particular visit, my daughter Sara and her boyfriend were enjoying speeding round and as I watched, I thought, 'I really must try it this time!' So my son Michael said he would drive me, and round we went. I was terrified; I sat huddled in the corner and shuddered with every jolt. I was really glad when the ride was over.

Later that evening, I was watching the cars again and I saw a woman my age driving in one on her own. She was whizzing round having a marvellous time and I suddenly thought, 'This is ridiculous! Here am I standing on the edge watching, and wishing that was me, but feeling too scared to make it happen. I'll do it!'

So I tried again, and this time I drove, and miraculously all my fears went and I had a wonderful time crashing into all the cars and laughing when I was bumped—instead of shuddering in the corner. I'll never be afraid of bumper cars again, and I realized what immense satisfaction there is for me in conquering a fear and doing joyfully the very thing I was so worried about. So if you have a fear that you know is stopping you doing the very things you have always wanted to do, even small things like going on bumper cars, remember this story, face the fear, and jump right in! You will be amazed at what you can do, and how powerful you really can be—if you let yourself.

4. Major fears

Returning now to really substantial fears, the sort that occur when we are placed in genuinely terrifying circumstances where our lives, homes, or loved ones are threatened: what can we do then? Understandably, in such situations, your saying to yourself 'I must let go of my fear!' may be the last thing you feel able to focus on, but I can only encourage you to try anyway. What we need to do also is learn how we can call upon the power of the Christ light to protect and uphold us, and truly lift us above the terror and distress.

It is amazing the way in which inner help and strength is always there when we really need it. But we do need to seek it. It can be as though a great ray of light reaches down and lifts the little self right into the strength of our courageous, shining self. The fact that the help is always there to be found, whatever we have to face, is an unfailing part of divine law.

I am thinking now of the evening when my father died very suddenly of a heart attack. All through the shock and trauma of that event, I felt in a way detached from my grieving little self and it was just as I have described: I felt lifted up by a ray of light which also helped me keep very steady and calm through the terrible moments of having to tell my mother. I now see that I fear of how we shall cope creates in our minds an unreal situation, because when the seeming tragedy does happen, it is never quite as we fear it might be because of the inner help we are given, as a result of what I think is best described as 'the grace of God'. I certainly found this during that critical time. All of us, all the family, were helped and uplifted in a wonderful way by the grace and love of God.

As well as having absolute trust in this process—trust in the ultimate goodness of God's plan for our life and the life of all those around us—we can also deliberately call on the power of the light to help and protect us.

CALLING ON THE POWER OF THE LIGHT TO HELP

Sometimes it is good to have an actual technique to summon the power of the light. Here is a simple inner ritual you can go through.

Picture yourself, or the person or place concerned, at the centre of a cross of light encircled by light, with the star shining

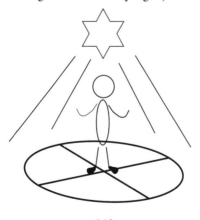

above and the rays of light from the star coming down to join the circle, as in the diagram, to make a wigwam of protection round you. In addition, see the sign of the cross of light encircled by light placed in front of the other person, or your house, or over your car—wherever is appropriate to the circumstances. Picture it like the shield of a knight of old. If you are protecting children, you can explain to them that you and they are being helped to use the magic power of the Christ light as a protection, like putting on a suit of armour.

This symbol of the cross of light encircled by light is one which we have used in the healing work of the White Eagle Lodge for many years and it is a very powerful protection. It was used on posters that were put up all over London during the second world war, with the words, 'The Forces of Darkness Halt! Before the Cross of Light', and it was found to have a remarkable effect then.*

WHAT TO DO WHEN YOU'RE IN THE MIDDLE OF A SITUATION WHICH BRINGS UP ALL YOUR FEARS

I have found that the first thing to do in an 'emergency' situation is this: affirm with all your heart and mind and soul that the light is all-powerful.

For example, say: *I trust in God and His perfect plan for my life.* It can help to keep on repeating this even as you face the fear head on. Repeat the affirmation, and encircle yourself with the light, as I have already described.

I had two opportunities to test if this works during my recent travels. On both occasions I had very real reason to fear for my

*See the book, THE STORY OF THE WHITE EAGLE LODGE (White Eagle Publishing Trust, 1986)

actual bodily safety. One was in broad daylight, when I was walking along a deserted beach and a passer-by, after asking me the time, snatched an imitation gold chain from my neck; fortunately he did not attack me further or take my bag. It all happened so quickly, but I did have a few moments to pray for help and afterwards I was filled with thankfulness that I had been protected by the light from anything worse happening.

The second incident was at nighttime when I thought two men were going to abduct me into their lorry. At the time, I felt almost detached from my little self and very calm. It was as though I was watching a film of myself and I 'knew' it would be all right in the end. I had time to ask for help and I did surround myself with the light. It really was an experience, but nothing bad did happen; suddenly the two men left me for no apparent reason, got back into their lorry and drove away. It was as though it had never happened, except as a test for me. I know that in my higher self I 'set up' both these incidents to test my courage and reinforce my trust in the protection of the light; and also, to remind me that I had to do my best to be sensible too, and look after myself. I love the saying, 'Allah will look after your camel, but first tie him to a tree'!

White Eagle teaches that we each have our own guardian angel whose work it is to ensure that nothing happens in our lives which is not a part of God's plan for our growth. In SPIRITUAL UNFOLDMENT I, he says:

> Every soul on earth is in the care of a guardian angel.... Your guardian angel never leaves you. From the moment of your entering upon mortal life to the time when you leave it, and even afterwards, your guardian angel is in touch with you. It is concerned with your karma and directs your life under the control of the lords of karma. The angel is impersonal in

151

the sense that its work is to see that you are guided towards opportunities to pay off karmic debts, or opportunities to earn good karma to add to the credit of your account. Thus every experience is an opportunity.

Your guardian angel is, further, a reminder that you aren't alone in these desperate circumstances.

WHAT TO DO WHEN YOUR FEAR WON'T GO AWAY

When your fear just will not go away—don't add that worry to the original one! Don't give it more energy by feeling bad, anxious or guilty. Sometimes we have to learn to live with fear for a while, and remain calm and trusting, even to act through it in spite of the fear, as I have described in the stories I have told. Sometimes the fear is there for a reason we cannot immediately understand. Don't hate it, or fight it—laugh at it if you can, and share it with others as you laugh. Tell people you feel afraid (though not in a heavy way) and then you won't feel so isolated, because others probably feel the same! A shared fear commiserated over and released into the area of laughter soon evaporates as positive companionship counteracts the negative thoughts. Choose carefully with whom you share your fear, and if possible let it be those who will lift you up into the Sunlight.

This leads us on to the question of patience, which is so closely linked with fear and trust, for if only we could truly trust in God's plan, as our master trusts, then we should find it easier to emulate the infinite patience of our master.

PATIENCE

Infinite patience is a difficult quality to find when you have both Sun and Mars in Aries, as I do! I learn the lesson of patience slowly. When I have an idea, I tend to want to act on it immediately and feel frustrated and held back if others want a longer time for reflection about it! I often expect others to be ready to go forward, or change, or do things more quickly than is right for them, and then feel impatient and irritable when everything moves along more slowly.

I had a good opportunity to learn this lesson of patience a few years ago when I was caught up in the worst traffic jam I have ever experienced. It was an extremely hot Friday afternoon and London's north circular road was at a standstill. There was no way of turning round as the carriageways were totally blocked in both directions, as well as in all the side-streets. The sun blazed relentlessly down; the traffic and buildings seemed to close in on me, and I started to have feelings of extreme claustrophobia, accompanied by nausea, headache, and dizziness. My little self wanted to get out of the heat of the car and run away, screaming that I could not stand it one moment longer. Then my true self started reminding me about what I had just been writing, that no matter what the problem, thinking of the star and breathing in its light always helps. So I did this and started saying the affirmation, *I am at peace: I trust in God.* I said this over and over again.

Almost immediately the panic feelings and attendant physical symptoms started to subside. Every time I remembered the appointment I was trying to get to, or how much I would prefer to be relaxing in my shady garden at that moment, I started to get the feelings coming back. Again, when I realized what was happening, I put my mind on the star and my affirmation. I had to do this many times over to uplift my little self. Then I started to visualize being by the lake of peace and enjoying the shade of cool pine trees and mountain breezes. Eventually I became totally centred in peace and able patiently to accept that I would be late (very hard for me) but that this was not the end of the world! Gradually the traffic jam sorted itself out and eventually I reached my destination. On reflection, I realized that none of the time had been wasted, for I had taken a real step forward in learning patience and how to make White Eagle's teaching really work in a testing situation.

Here is a final thought on what to do if everything seems to go wrong. One of my favourite sayings in THE QUIET MIND is the one headed 'Just Laugh!' (p. 91) and reminds us of the great value of a sense of humour. To be able to laugh helps in so many difficult situations. White Eagle himself, as I have already said, has a wonderful sense of humour and beautiful, twinkling eyes. He makes jokes and laughs and encourages us to be light-hearted. In one teaching given many years ago, he actually referred to the '*jolly* masters'! Our elder brethren in the world of light do not want us to go around being serious and overly pious all the time. They want us to have lots of fun and laughs, and allow God's happiness to flood through our whole being. I find that every single time I have made an effort to step through a fear, taken a risk and set out on an adventure, it has opened the way to some of the most joyous and significant experiences of my whole life. Fear and impatience close the door on life's experiences. Trust and confidence in God's plan allow the miracles to happen, and happiness to fill our lives. So let us all follow White Eagle's words in the first chapter of the book:

> Walk each day in childlike faith, with your hand clasped in the hand of your Master. That hand is the hand of truth, it is security, it will never fail you. Earthly men may fail you but never your Master. (p. 17)

THE SIX-POINTED STAR (9)

All things work together for good for the man who loves God. They must do, because he puts himself en rapport with God and then everything is good. (p. 92)

Being trusting. The upward-pointing triangle stands for the simple child of God, giving his or her complete trust to Father–Mother God and the divine plan.

God's love and light: the omnipotence of divine Law. When the child of God gives complete love and trust to God, the full glory of the light can totally transform and illumine the soul's life—the downward triangle.

Happiness. A soul who is thus illumined is truly happy and can face any condition without fear.

A MEDITATION ON 'A MASTER SOUL IS PATIENT, TRUSTING IN GOD'S GOODNESS AND HIS PERFECT PLAN'

Live every moment, every hour, every day, tranquilly in the protective love of God. (p. 88)

Say, out loud if possible, *I .... (insert your name) let go all my fears. I trust in God and in His perfect plan for my life.* (You may like to say it a number of times.)

In your imagination, take your teacher's hand and come with him/her, along the sunlit path to the lake of peace. As you walk together along the path, open your heart to him/her. Talk about all the things which are troubling you.... He/she understands totally, and being able to share your fears helps you let them go.... Maybe you actually take off your back a 'pack' of fears and watch it disintegrate in the sunlight; or watch the fears float away and dissolve in the water as you sit together by the lake.

As you watch the sunlight reflected by the still water, it is easy to absorb the peace into your whole being, including your little self, which perhaps was so troubled and anxious.... Feel more and more of your troubles melting in the sunlight, and in their place you can breathe in renewed trust in God and in His perfect plan for your life. There can be no mistake. Divine Law works unfailingly and everything is just, perfect and true.

After this time of peaceful contemplation, your teacher takes your hand and you feel new strength flowing into you and new lightness in your heart. You know that he/she will help you have the courage to take any action on the outer planes which is needed, and that you will always be enfolded in his/her strong and loving support. It folds round you now, in a warm healing cloak, as you walk back to your earth life.

AFFIRMATIONS (9)

I am patient
I trust in God and in His perfect plan for my life
I am divine patience
I am divine trust
I .... (insert your name) let go all my fears
I put my hand in the hand of the master
I am strong in the light of the star
The forces of darkness Halt! before the Cross of Light
All is well
Underneath me are the everlasting arms
I am divine happiness.

A FEW FINAL WORDS

Writing this book has been both a joyous and a growing 'journey' for me. In the preparation of every chapter, and at every stage, I have been challenged in my own personal life, and tested as to how much I could actually put into practice myself. Sometimes I have succeeded, sometimes I have not done so well, but I have tried, as White Eagle says, to 'keep on keeping on' and been sustained throughout by his teaching, and in particular by THE QUIET MIND.

I hope this book will help you also to keep on keeping on and be a useful companion for you on your own journey.

With my love,

Jenny Dent